The Thing Itself

Essays on Academics and the State

Michael C. Munger

February 2015

◊◊◊

Mungerella Publishing

ADVANCE PRAISE FOR
THE THING ITSELF

PJ O'Rourke, Author of *ON THE WEALTH OF NATIONS: BOOKS THAT CHANGED THE WORLD*:

◊ *"How did you get this email address?"*

Arturo, Miami Gate Agent for Delta Airlines:

◊ *"Todo lo que dice de mí es verdadero. Y este tipo tiene cero comprensión de 'la mente Latina.' Idiota."*

Dr. Timothy Groseclose, Professor at George Mason University and Author of *LEFT TURN: HOW LIBERAL MEDIA BIAS DISTORTS THE AMERICAN MIND:*

◊ *"I laughed, I cried...It was...it was better than C*A*T*S."*

Dr. Russ Roberts, Hoover Institution, Author of *HOW ADAM SMITH CAN CHANGE YOUR LIFE* and Host of ECONTALK:

◊ *"Mike Munger is the world's foremost scholar of unicorns. Read this book and you'll understand how people can smell the strawberries."*

LONDON LEDGER-TRIBUNE:

◊ *"Blatant rubbish....tasteless nonsense..."*

Donna Gingerella, Esq., Wife of the Author, On Many Occasions:

◊ *"You aren't funny. You think you're funny, but you're not."*

Copyedited & Designed by
Kathrin DePue, The Writing Mechanic

Dedicated to
Donna Gingerella
...the best thing in my life.

In vain you tell me that Artificial Government is good, but that I fall out only with the Abuse. The Thing! *the Thing itself* is the abuse! Observe, my Lord, I pray you, that grand Error upon which all artificial legislative power is founded. It was observed, that Men had ungovernable Passions, which made it necessary to guard against the Violence they might offer to each other. They appointed governors over them for this Reason; but a worse and more perplexing Difficulty arises, how to be defended against the Governors?

—Edmund Burke, *A Vindication of Natural Society* 1982 [1756], pp. 64-65 (emphasis added)

TABLE OF CONTENTS

PREFACE

If you spend a lot of time watching people, you will notice three tendencies in how they think about government and policy. The first is that most of us, in each generation, think our problems are unique and more difficult than in times past. Second, we tend to claim credit for what we see as successes and blame others, or bad luck, for what we see as failures. Third, we think every problem has a simple cause (even if it doesn't), and we should "do something," even if we shouldn't.

Of course, our problems *are* unique, in every unimportant way. The central problem, though, is constant: how can we get large groups of people to work together to achieve the enormous mutual and individual benefits that come from cooperating peacefully? Sure, it is perfectly true that the particular obstacles to peace and cooperation are always changing. But the core problem is the same: we're all in this together, just like always.

The second tendency really causes a lot of difficulties, and I think it's because of what Thomas Hobbes called "vainglory," as in, "The passion whose violence or continuance maketh madness is either great vainglory, which is commonly called pride and self-conceit, or great dejection of mind." My modern update of that is, "Success is pure skill, as any winner will tell you; failure is bad luck, as any loser will tell you." Either way, that kind of oversimplification maketh madness and always has.

Finally, the "we should do something!" fallacy...gosh. Shamans of old could wield enormous power over the gullible if they could predict something like a storm, or—better—a lunar eclipse. "This very evening, the Night Wolf will devour the Moon Virgin! But if you pay me many coins of silver, I will force Night Wolf to cough the Moon Virgin back up, unharmed!" P.J. O'Rourke used a version of that story 20 years ago to describe fundraising letters from Greenpeace, but it could just as well have been a description of fundraising letters from the Heritage Foundation. Fear sells, and pretending to be able to solve problems sells even better. The real problem is that fear-selling has metastasized. Now the shamans work for the government. But it's not the government's fault; it's our fault. The folks at the National Security Agency, the Environmental Protection Agency, and the Transportation Security Administration are just giving the people what they want.

Parsing it as if it were logical, it works like this:

1. X is a problem.

2. We should do something

3. Y is something.

4. Therefore, we should do Y.

5. If Y does not solve X, it must mean we didn't do enough Y, and we need to do more.

The problems here are pretty clear. Step 2 is pretty weak, as many times we should not do something, but the step from 3 to 4 is nonsense. Things are rarely so bad that demagogues can't make them worse. Given the problems of deciding that "we" should "do" Y, 5 is complete nonsense.

Imagine you have a six-year-old daughter, and that she has 'nervous fever,' or what today we would call typhoid. It's 1755, and we don't understand germs or fevers very well. Still, you love your daughter, and you can't just sit around. You call the doctor, and the doctor comes to the house. "Please, do something. Do *something* to help my daughter!" you say.

Now, if the doctor were a good 1700s doctor, he would say, "We don't really know much about fevers. It's better if we just try to make her comfortable, cool her head with compresses, and let it run its course." But if he said that, *you would find another doctor*! You are scared. You want him to do something.

THE THING ITSELF

◇◇◇◇◇◇◇◇◇◇◇◇◇◇◇

That *something* in 1755 was a combination of bleeding and a glyster. A glyster involved the introduction of that new wonder drug, tobacco, into the lower bowel because the medicos thought it would be absorbed faster that way. Yes, that means exactly what you think it means: The doctor used a bellows to make sure that the tobacco smoke made it into...well, you know.

Then the doctor--the one you hired because he promised to do something--takes out a lancet, and makes a small incision in your daughter's wrist. The theory was that the fever was in the blood itself, and bleeding was the only treatment doctors knew, other than the tobacco smoke thing. Not surprisingly, people thought that fevers were deadly, and to be fair, fevers really were deadly...if someone panicked and called a doctor to do something.

Of course, your daughter doesn't get better; she gets worse. Your daughter's fever is still very high, so the earnest quack takes another half-pint of blood. And another.

Then she dies. And then you blame the doctor for not having been active enough. He didn't really try! He could have saved her! The idea that it was your fear and your panicked insistence of "we ought to do something" that killed your daughter....well, that never occurs to you.

What does this story have to do with our contemporary problems—in a time when we know how to treat a 'nervous fever'? If in the above story you switch the setting from your house to the nation, it's pretty much the same problem. We may know how to treat fevers, but we still don't know much about economics. If there is a recession, the only thing our politicos know to do is the fiscal version of what the medicos did in the 18th century: They bleed the patient by expanding the size of the government sector. Oh, and the 'stimulus' and those shovel-ready projects? If that's not blowing smoke up someone's bum, I don't know what is. And when it doesn't work, Paul Krugman says he knew it wouldn't work because we did not *do enough* of it.

We haven't really come so far since the 18th century after all. We have about the same level understanding of macroeconomic policy problems now that doctors had about fevers then. The best we can hope for is that the 'treatment' will fail to kill the patient outright. Given our lack of understanding, the best thing we could do is nothing—other than try to make the symptoms a little less painful. But any economist who says that gets fired, and you people panic and hire some quack who advises an immediate treatment. Next thing you know, the

THE THING ITSELF

◇◇◇◇◇◇◇◇◇◇◇◇◇◇◇

government is pumping those bellows like crazy. Enjoy your monetary glyster.

The essays in this book were written at various times between 2003 and 2014, and address my experiences in academics. going back to 1986 I have separated them into two groups: focusing on the state as a thing with its own goals and values, and on academic politics. In writing them, I felt a bit like a *fin de millennium* Forrest Gump—present purely by accident at the time and place in the background of some important events. My goal has been to laugh at these events, and at myself, as a way of understanding them better. In reading, I'm not sure you'll think you understand more, but I do hope you'll laugh.

I don't mean to sound a note of pessimism, unless it's pessimistic to expect the worst and think it will never get better. I'd prefer to think that "not very good" is the best we can hope for from the state and take a little more humility into the way that we analyze our policy problems.

Let's play a favorite game of academics: Who wrote this?

[Democracy] is always in the position of a ship without a commander. In such a ship, if fear of the enemy, or the occurrence of a storm induce the crew to be of one mind

6

and to obey the helmsman, everything goes well; but if they recover from this fear, and begin to treat their officers with contempt, and to quarrel with each other because they are no longer all of one mind,—one party wishing to continue the voyage, and the other urging the steersman to bring the ship to anchor; some letting out the sheets, and others hauling them in, and ordering the sails to be furled,—their discord and quarrels make a sorry show to lookers on; and the position of affairs is full of risk to those on board engaged on the same voyage; and the result has often been that, after escaping the dangers of the widest seas, and the most violent storms, they wreck their ship in harbour and close to shore.

The answer is Polybius in *Histories*, Book VI, Chapter 44. It was written around 130 B.C.E., almost exactly 2050 years ago, but it's a terrific description of our experience in transitioning from George W. Bush to Barack Obama. I hope I can convince you that the problems we face with government are not unique—that we are not in trouble simply because we have a bad person at the helm and need a better helmsman. The state can only govern through fear, and if that fear is unjustified, the state is forced to

THE THING ITSELF
◇◇◇◇◇◇◇◇◇◇◇◇◇◇◇

manufacture it through political dumb shows, like Dick Cheney speeches and TSA body searches. We overestimate the size of the problems we face because the state needs us to think it is protecting us from certain abuses.

But the *thing*, the thing *itself*, is the abuse.

1. INTRODUCTION: Seeing Unicorns

I started this book for fun, but it quickly became serious. But then again, we do live in serious times. The American education system is reaping what it has sown: generations of students now becoming teachers, who didn't learn to think and were never taught how to learn.

Me? I blame the state. Not the state of North Carolina (where I live and which I like very much) and not the nation of the United States (which has tottered along the razor's edge dividing tyranny from chaos as well as any nation ever has). No, my blame lies with the sirens' song of the state—the blind faith the idea of the state inspires in otherwise bright and pragmatic people. The state as it could be, as it is in their minds, is the problem. It's like a horror movie where the smartest character goes into a trance and then, staring sightlessly, says in a spooky voice: "I...see...unicorns!"

The State as Unicorn

Unicorns, of course, are fabulous horse-like creatures with a large spiraling horn on their foreheads. They eat rainbows but can go without eating for years if necessary. They can carry enormous amounts of cargo without tiring, and their flatulence

THE THING ITSELF

◇◇◇◇◇◇◇◇◇◇◇◇◇◇

smells like pure, fresh strawberries—so riding behind one in a wagon is a pleasure.

For all these reasons, unicorns are ideal pack animals; in fact, they may be the key to improving human society and sharing prosperity.

To the uninitiated, it might appear that there is a fatal flaw in the above argument because (making air quotes now) unicorns do not "actually exist." But that's incorrect: The existence of unicorns is easily proven. Close your eyes. Now envision a unicorn. The one I see is white, with an orange-colored horn. The unicorn is surrounded by rainbows (perhaps it's time for lunch). Your vision may look slightly different, but there is no question that when I say "unicorn," the picture in your mind corresponds fairly closely to the picture in my mind. So *unicorns do exist*; we can see them, and we have a shared conception of what they are.

When I am discussing politics with someone, it's often not long before I realize they see unicorns. My friends generally dislike politicians, find democracy messy and distasteful, and object to the brutality and coercive excesses of foreign wars, the war on drugs, the brutality of police tactics, and the spying of the NSA. But their solution is, without exception, to expand the power of "the state." That seems like literal insanity to me, a non sequitur of such monstrous proportions that I have trouble taking it seriously...

...until I realized that they want a kind of unicorn: a state that has the properties, motivations, knowledge, and abilities that they can imagine for it. When I finally realized that we were talking past each other, I felt somewhat dumb. Essentially this very realization—that people who favor expansion of government imagine a state different from the one possible in the physical world—has been a core part of the argument made by classical liberals for at least three hundred years.

The problem in the minds of many people is that we have just happened to choose bad people or improper systems. Come the next election, we'll have a Messiah! The next reform will lead to Utopia! No. No, we won't, and it won't.

Adam Smith made a trenchant observation about people who see unicorns:

> It is the system of government, the situation in which [people] are placed, that I mean to censure, not the character of those who have acted in it. They acted as their situation naturally directed, and they who have

THE THING ITSELF

◇◇◇◇◇◇◇◇◇◇◇◇◇◇◇

> *clamoured the loudest against them would probably not*
> *have acted better themselves.*

Smith was talking about the employees of the East India
Company in this passage, but the insight is a general one: when
a system fails, the cause generally arises from the contradictory
incentives, the logic of action, or the unanticipated consequences
inherent *in that system*. Blaming the people is a mistake. The
people who work in that system probably act in much the same
way that other people would act if they found themselves in that
system. So while it's true that one can imagine a state that works
differently, there are no actual human beings who can work in
that system and deliver what statists can imagine.

    People imagine that the police in Ferguson, Missouri
who shot Michael Brown were bad men; the cop who put the
chokehold on Erik Garner must have been evil. But that's not
true: those policemen reacted the way that most other people
would have reacted, had they similar experiences and a similar
situation. The use of force is the essence of the state and the logic
of the state, and you would want it that way. The alternative, as
Thomas Hobbes argued in *Leviathan*, would be chaos and
revolution. The state must wield enough force to overawe

resistance and to crush non-compliance. These acts of violence are not abuses: they are the thing itself.

Friedrich Hayek, who won the Nobel Prize in Economics in 1974, apparently met many folks who saw unicorns. In his book *The Fatal Conceit*, he said, "The curious task of economics is to demonstrate to men how little they really know about what they *imagine* they can design." (emphasis added)

I have a solution to the unicorns problem. I call it, immodestly, "the Munger Test."

The Munger Test

People immediately understand why relying on imaginary creatures would be a problem for planners working to design practical mass transit. But they may not immediately see why "the state" that they can imagine is a unicorn. My suggestion:

1. Go ahead; make your argument for what you want the state to do and what you want the state to be in charge of.

2. Then, go back and look at your statement. Everywhere you said "the state," white that out and replace it with "politicians I actually know, running in electoral systems with voters and interest groups that actually exist."

3. If you still believe your statement, then we have something to talk about.

This leads to loads of fun, believe me. When someone says, "The State should be in charge of hundreds of thousands of heavily armed troops, with the authority to use that coercive power." Ask them to take out the unicorn ("The State") and replace it with George W. Bush or, maybe, Ted Cruz. Do you still believe the claim?

If someone says, "The State should be able to choose subsidies and taxes to change the incentives people face in deciding what energy sources to use," ask them to remove "The State" and replace it with "Senators from states that rely on coal, oil, or corn-ethanol for income." Still sound like a good idea?

How about, "The State should make rules for regulating sales of high performance electric cars." Now, the switch: "Representatives from Michigan and other states that produce parts for internal combustion engines should be in charge of regulating Tesla Motors out of existence." Gosh, maybe not...

The problem, of course, is that the unicorn people *imagine*—whether it's a government, a bureaucracy, or a police force—is wise, benevolent, and omnipotent. In some sense, of course, they are right because when they close their eyes they really can see the unicorn and maybe even smell the strawberries.

Of course, the problem is larger than I have made it seem so far. Market advocates can be just as imaginative as statists. "Free market" zealots have analogous blind spots and are just as capable of dismissing disasters, such as the Deepwater Horizon spill or the housing bubble, rather than accepting the fact that markets fail, too.

Alternatively, the problem may not be as bad as I've made it out to be. There are plenty of politicians and government officials who really do care about the public, or at least about their vision of the "public interest." They are not selfish and often work long careers at rates of pay less than they could get in the private sector because they care deeply about their jobs. Still, that was likely true about Torquemada and the other leaders of the Spanish Inquisition in 1485. The point is, a desire to "do good" can be just as terrifying as officials who are lazy or corrupt.

All of this reminds me of an old joke, which has probably been around for a long time but that I first heard from Gordon Tullock, the famous Public Choice economist. It seems there was a county fair in a rural area at which they had a "beautiful pig" contest. Adult pigs aren't very pretty, and so there were only two entrants. The judges sat down, and the first pig was brought out. And it was *ugly*! The judges recoil in horror; the pig is muddy, smelly, and hairy. Yuck.

They confer and announce that they are giving the beauty prize to the second pig.

Of course, they haven't seen the second pig, but that first pig was so ugly that the second one must be better, right? At least, they imagine that it must be better because they have actually seen how ugly the first pig was.

Far too many of our policy debates, on both sides, are conducted in much the same way those judges decided the beautiful pig contest. The answer is either "free markets" or "state control," with no middle ground. The best argument for a presumption in favor of markets can't be that we *imagine* markets functioning perfectly because we could also imagine states functioning perfectly. The best argument for a presumption in favor of private action is, in my opinion, an honest look at how ugly the state is. Market failures only justify state action if, as an empirical matter, state action is an improvement. Bringing out that ugly market pig and then giving the prize to the state we can only imagine is generally going to result in failure. So long as pro-market advocates insist that our opponents are mistaken about the properties of "The State"—*which doesn't exist in the first place*, at least not in the way that statists imagine—then we will lose the attention of many sympathetic people who are primarily interested in consequences. The problem is that most citizens understand very little about what the state that they imagine can actually do.

I Was A Unicorn Rider

I started graduate school as a Maoist. My office mate and I read Mao's "little red book" just to piss people off. We also had a large Soviet flag right up on one whole wall, where everyone could see it. This was 1980, and the Soviet Union was real. I wasn't, but it was.

Being a radical socialist was darned fun, and we got lots of attention, in a juvenile "stick their pigtails in the inkwell" way. But to live in that fairyland, you have to suppress your reason and senses. So after about four months, my office mate and I separately, and quietly, dismounted from our unicorns.

I can't understand why so many people in academics get stuck at "Step 1: Socialist Utopian Nutjob." Arrested intellectual development should signal failure, but we give them endowed chairs and call such people "theorists": literary theorists, social

17

theorists, theoretical theorists, and theorists of the practice of theoretical theory.

Ludwig von Mises said this really cool thing in *Epistemological Problems of Economics*. He said:

> *Scarcely anyone interests himself in social problems without being led to do so by the desire to see reforms enacted. In almost all cases, before anyone begins to study the science, he has already decided on definite reforms that he wants to put through. Only a few have the strength to accept the knowledge that these reforms are impracticable and to draw all the inferences from it. Most men endure the sacrifice of the intellect more easily than the sacrifice of their daydreams. They cannot bear that their utopias should run aground on the unalterable necessities of human existence. What they yearn for is another reality different from the one given in this world...They wish to be free of a universe of whose order they do not approve.*

And that's what socialist "theory" is: an alternative universe—a happy place where laws of economics (resources are scarce, producing things takes work, governments cannot create value) and possibly even physics (all roads should be downhill because in my mind that would be better) don't apply.

Between my Maoism in 1980 and my current position as Director of Duke's Philosophy, Politics, and Economics Program, I encountered a menagerie of academic fauna, with freakish adaptations to local conditions. In the course of the past 30 years, I taught at Dartmouth, University of Texas-Austin, University of North Carolina-Chapel Hill, and then Duke, starting in 1997. My state-skeptic views are as strange to most academics as if I were a cannibal or a Zoroastrian dastur, or worse, actually, since those guys would at least be multicultural and romantically primitive.

In those 30 years, the American academy has been transformed. Where the left was once outré, it is now tiredly and firmly entrenched *inside*. Because of this hegemony, many faculty on the left have softened into baccate self-caricatures, unable to tolerate dissent and unwilling to think hard enough to justify their own positions.

Ironically, the flaccid left now exemplifies many of the qualities it (rightly) despised in the hidebound "conservative" administrations whom the then-radicals, now-faculty fought against in their salad days.

THE THING ITSELF

◇◇◇◇◇◇◇◇◇◇◇◇◇◇◇

Still, there is cause for optimism. College is, or could be, a consumer-driven business. If real classes, with real content, are offered, students will flock to them. In the pages that follow, I try to describe some of the experiences I have had while thinking about policy problems in an academic setting. I don't mean to be disrespectful because the institutions of education have my greatest respect, but sometimes things that happen just have to be told.

Michael Munger

◊◊◊◊◊◊◊◊◊◊◊◊◊

THE STATE

THE THING ITSELF

◊◊◊◊◊◊◊◊◊◊◊◊◊◊

2. THE THING ITSELF: The State

If you call someone a "bureaucrat," it comes across as an epithet. A bureaucrat is someone with no imagination who insists on following rules and regulations. Here is an example of someone who many people might call a "bureaucrat": Cherrail Curry-Hagler of the DC Transit Police.

The following facts, at least according to the *Washington Post,* July 30, 2004, are indisputable: About 6:30 p.m. on 16 July, 2004 Stephanie Willett, a 45 year old EPA scientist, was riding the escalator down from 11th Street NW to the subway station, and eating a "PayDay" candy bar. Cherrail Curry-Hagler, DC transit policewoman (and possible bureaucrat), was riding up on the other escalator. It should be noted that there is a rule against eating on the Metro in the District of Columbia. Officer Curry-Hagler warned Willett to finish the candy before entering the station.

Willett nodded. But she kept chewing the PayDay as she walked through the fare gates. Curry-Hagler, who had turned around and followed Willett, warned her again as she stuffed the last bit into her mouth before throwing the wrapper into the trash can near the station manager's kiosk. Curry-Hagler ordered Willett to stop and show ID. Willett refused and retorted, "Why

THE THING ITSELF

◇◇◇◇◇◇◇◇◇◇◇◇◇◇◇

don't you go and take care of some real crime?" Admittedly, this may have seemed rude, since her mouth was still full of PayDay bar. The scientist rode a second escalator down to catch her Orange Line train.

At this point, according to citizen Willett, the officer grabbed her and searched her, running her hands under Willett's bra and around her waist. She put Willett into the back seat of a police car, took her to the 1st District station, and locked her in a cell. At 9:30 p.m., after she paid a $10 fee, Willett was released to her husband.

To review, here are facts to consider:

- Ms. Willett was on a DOWN ESCALATOR. She couldn't turn around.
- She was already chewing the candy bar. She couldn't spit it out without littering, and spit-out-candy is pretty nasty litter.
- When Willett got to the bottom of the escalator, she put the last bit into her mouth, threw the wrapper into the trash can, and continued on toward her train.

There is no way that Ms. Willett could have better obeyed the instruction not to eat in the station, unless she had run back up the escalator or spit out the candy bar. On the other hand, and in

24

defense of the bureaucrat/policewoman, given the laws on the books, Ms. Willett had committed a crime. You can't take food into a station, and you can't eat in the station. It's the law. The law says: *"It is unlawful to eat, drink, or smoke in the Metro system because of the labor and cost associated with maintaining the cleanliness of the transportation system as well as for safety reasons. Customers can be cited by Metro Transit Police for violating the no eating, no drinking, and no smoking rules."*

Let's step back a moment. One very good reason to use bureaucracy, and bureaucrats, is what legal scholars call "equal protection." The rules apply to everyone, and good bureaucrats apply the law to everyone equally. So the officer had not, in fact, abused the system; Ms. Curry-Hagler, and all the other Transit Police in DC, are supposed to keep their gimlet eyes peeled for offenses *exactly* like these. Whether there should be such a law against eating is an interesting question, but that is not for the police, whose job it is to *enforce* the law, to ask.

People often object when a bureaucrat does his or her job. You think that's wrong? Consider these: The TSA employees who makes my kid take off his shoes at the airport and who makes me show my boarding pass four times:

bureaucrat. The counter guy at the Department of Motor Vehicles who refuses to process my application for a driver's license because I forgot my Social Security card: bureaucrat. The municipal building inspector who makes me tear out a row of newly planted shrubs so he can visually check the direction and the depth of the new sewer line and the concrete footings on the posts of my screen porch: bureaucrat. We hire bureaucrats to do very specific jobs, and then we get mad at them for doing it.

Is there an alternative to these examples of zealous pettiness? Sure. We could give discretion to bureaucrats and the police to enforce the laws they like and ignore the rest. "Pick those rules you like, and the people you don't like, and make only those people obey those rules; your choice." That approach would clearly be a ticket on the train to tyranny and corruption. Discretion allows the representative of the state to indulge racism, or sadism, or whatever-ism. So we are stuck with rules and regulations that *must be* foolishly blunt and mindlessly enforced by bureaucrats. Bureaucracy is the nature of government, not a perversion of it. You can't have all those laws, a strong presumption in favor of the state's truthfulness, and expect to protect the weak. As always, Bastiat said it best, and most succinctly:

When under the pretext of fraternity, the legal code imposes mutual sacrifices on the citizens, human nature is not thereby abrogated. Everyone will then direct his efforts toward contributing little to, and taking much from, the common fund of sacrifices. Now, is it the most unfortunate who gains from this struggle? Certainly not, but rather the most influential and calculating.

The system is not "designed" to help the poor. Of course police officers are going to use excessive force, and of course police officers are going to have and act on racial and class-based preferences. Then, the system—in the courts, the prosecutor's office, and the grand jury—is going to protect itself. That's the system, unless you believe in unicorns. The system is designed to protect the system, and it does that very well, so it's well designed. If the left were serious about helping the poor, they would recognize that the only answer is much less of the system.

The solution? Fewer laws. We have criminalized so many behaviors that we have given the police an impossibly large and complicated task. Unavoidably, this comes with substantial latitude to act on prejudice, bigotry, and simple anger. But let's be clear: the police, in their defense, have an impossible job. They have come to see almost everyone around them, everyday, as a lawbreaker and a danger to society. Harvey Silvergate famously estimated that most of us commit at least three felonies per day. The only thing that prevents us from being jailed is the discretion and public spiritedness of the prosecutor.

But what if you don't want to have to rely on the discretion and public spiritedness of the prosecutor? I'd rather rely on the fact, and it is a fact that I haven't actually done anything wrong, and therefore the laws that could be used to charge me with felonies shouldn't exist in the first place. More and more, our government's motto when it comes to citizens is "trust, but terrify." As long as the left (with the active complicity of the non-libertarian right) continues to criminalize being black or poor, it's not surprising that the police will continue to treat poor people as criminals. That's not because poor people really are criminals; it's simply because, statistically, many criminals are poor. The police have to ration their effort and attention, so they use heuristics and short-cuts. If we rely on the discretion of the police, the poor suffer.

Discretion is Bad: Guarding the Guardians

Around 100 C.E., the Roman satirist Juvenal wrote about a problem of making sure someone does the right thing, even if the boss isn't watching. His example (it was, after all, a satire) focused on ensuring the sexual fidelity of wives:

> *I know well the advice and warnings of my old friends—*
> *'Put on a lock and keep your wife guarded indoors.' Yes,*
> *but who is to guard the guardians? They get paid in kind*
> *for holding their tongues as to their young lady's*
> *escapades; participation seals their lips. The wily wife*
> *arranges accordingly and begins with them...* (Satire #6)

Juvenal's question, *"Quis custodiet ipsos custodes?"* ("Who will guard the guardians?") is the problem that bureaucracy solves, but it is also a problem that a reliance on bureaucracy creates. Bureaucracy is a form of organization characterized by three features:

1. Hierarchy, or subordination to the authority of rules and procedures, giving the bureaucrat limited personal discretion for action.

2. The absence of any direct fee for service arrangement for pay, and difficulty in defining or measuring the precise output of the bureaucrat. As a consequence, bureaucrats are generally paid and promoted based on inputs alone, including credentials such as advanced degrees, or on seniority and time in rank.

3. Protection of tenure, meaning that the bureaucrat cannot easily be removed from office and, then, only for clearly defined reasons.

It is tempting to think that democracy is the way government works. To some extent, it is true that democratic processes are how legislatures make decisions, and allocate resources, in making budgetary and policy choices. But the implementation of policy, and the administration of government, is done everywhere almost exclusively through systems of bureaucracy.

Bureaucracies are the only means by which equal protection, and equal treatment, can be assured. Not that this is always a good thing: In your job, you may be a CEO. When you go to bars, people may flock around you because of your charm and good looks. But when you stand in line at the Post Office, or at the Department of Motor Vehicles, you are just a number, waiting for your turn. Your case will be decided, if the bureaucrat is doing her job, strictly based on the rules and regulations, rather than on your status, wealth, or power.

All of this suggests a fundamental question, one that we have to answer before we can continue. If we all dislike bureaucracy, and insult bureaucrats, why is this form of organization so dominant? Why do we choose to have unelected officials in such positions of power, and what kinds of institutional designs can keep that power in check? Who will guard the guardians?

Guardians

In Plato's *Republic*, 500 years before Juvenal wrote his satires, the problem is solved in a rather disturbing way (though this may also be satire). Near the end of Book III, it is asked of Socrates, "How is the society to be protected from the Guardians [the Rulers of the society]?":

> *[P]erhaps the word 'guardian' in the fullest sense ought to be applied to this higher class only who preserve us against foreign enemies and maintain peace among our citizens at home, that the one may not have the will, or the others the power, to harm us. The young men whom we before called guardians may be more properly designated auxiliaries and supporters of the principles of the rulers.*
>
> *I agree with you, he said.*

THE THING ITSELF
◊◊◊◊◊◊◊◊◊◊◊◊◊◊◊

How then may we devise one of those needful falsehoods of which we lately spoke—just one royal lie which may deceive the rulers, if that be possible, and at any rate the rest of the city?

What sort of lie? he said.

Nothing new, I replied; only an old Phoenician tale of what has often occurred before now in other places, (as the poets say, and have made the world believe,) though not in our time, and I do not know whether such an event could ever happen again, or could now even be made probable, if it did.

How your words seem to hesitate on your lips!

You will not wonder, I replied, at my hesitation when you have heard.

Speak, he said, and fear not.

◇◇◇◇◇◇◇◇◇◇◇◇◇

Well then, I will speak, although I really know not how to look you in the face, or in what words to utter the audacious fiction, which I propose to communicate gradually, first to the rulers, then to the soldiers, and lastly to the people. They are to be told that their youth was a dream, and the education and training which they received from us, an appearance only; in reality during all that time they were being formed and fed in the womb of the earth, where they themselves and their arms and appurtenances were manufactured; when they were completed, the earth, their mother, sent them up; and so, their country being their mother and also their nurse, they are bound to advise for her good, and to defend her against attacks, and her citizens they are to regard as children of the earth and their own brothers.

You had good reason, he said, to be ashamed of the lie which you were going to tell.

True, I replied, but there is more coming; I have only told you half. Citizens, we shall say to them in our tale, you are brothers, yet God has framed you differently. Some

THE THING ITSELF

of you have the power of command, and in the composition of these he has mingled gold, wherefore also they have the greatest honour; others he has made of silver, to be auxillaries; others again who are to be husbandmen and craftsmen he has composed of brass and iron; and the species will generally be preserved in the children. But as all are of the same original stock, a golden parent will sometimes have a silver son, or a silver parent a golden son. And God proclaims as a first principle to the rulers, and above all else, that there is nothing which should so anxiously guard, or of which they are to be such good guardians, as of the purity of the race. They should observe what elements mingle in their offspring; for if the son of a golden or silver parent has an admixture of brass and iron, then nature orders a transposition of ranks, and the eye of the ruler must not be pitiful towards the child because he has to descend in the scale and become a husbandman or artisan, just as there may be sons of artisans who having an admixture of gold or silver in them are raised to honour, and become guardians or auxiliaries. For an oracle says that when a man of brass or iron guards the State, it will be destroyed. Such is the tale; is there any possibility of making our citizens believe in it?

Not in the present generation, he replied; there is no way of accomplishing this; but their sons may be made to believe in the tale, and their sons' sons, and posterity after them.

I see the difficulty, I replied; yet the fostering of such a belief will make them care more for the city and for one another.

Philosophers and political scientists refer to this section as the Platonic "Noble Lie." It is a way of solving the "Who Will Guard the Guardians?" problem: tell the rulers that they have to serve the people, and follow the rules, because God—or our secular god, the State—said so. Prophetically, Plato also reveals the concern with "purity of the race" that collectivism so devolves into.

In the late Enlightenment period, in the 18th century, it became unacceptable for leaders to invoke God as the ruler or the justification for rules. After the French Revolution, bureaucrats turned to the State itself as the object of loyalty and to professional codes of ethics as guides to behavior. The modern version of the "Noble Lie" is told to all of us, every day: The reason we have powerful governments is that the people in government are working not for themselves but for the people.

We don't need to "guard the guardians"; with the right rules, they will guard themselves, and their guard duty will actually be fun because they will get to ride unicorns. Having set up the problem this way, we will now turn to a discussion of the nature of purely bureaucratic forms of organization.

Bureaucracy: The Rules, All the Rules, and Only the Rules

Wilhelm von Humboldt is famous for founding the modern German university system, after which most other universities have been modeled. He is also famous for his observations on the intellectual opportunity cost of organizing bureaucratic activities:

> *We must not overlook here one particular harmful consequence, since it so closely affects human development; and this is that the administration of political affairs itself becomes in time so full of complications that it requires an incredible number of*

persons to devote their time to its supervision, in order that it may not fall into utter confusion. Now, by far the greater portion of these have to deal with the mere symbols and formulas of things; and thus, not only are men of first-rate capacity withdrawn from anything which gives scope for thinking, and useful hands are diverted from real work, but their intellectual powers themselves suffer from this partly empty, partly narrow employment. (pp. 29-30)

This is a really interesting point: being a bureaucrat, a really good bureaucrat, is hard. Knowledge of the rules, and fair and uniform application of the rules, requires long study and real dedication.

But if the social benefits to the efforts required to pass a civil service exam are negligible, then the job of well-paid bureaucrat is simply a "rent"—an artificially created bonus, the competition for which will dissipate resources, just as Humboldt pointed out. This is one danger of bureaucratic organization, since the actual social benefits created by the position are hard to measure or gauge. Suppose, for example, that someone decides that teachers will be paid more if they get a master's degree. Then many teachers will spend the time and money to get a master's degree, even if the actual improvement in the quality of their teaching is negligible.

This raises again the question: what is so good about bureaucracy? To learn the answer, it is useful to examine the thoughts of the great advocate of bureaucratic organization, the German sociologist and social theorist, Max Weber.

Weber's account is interesting. These other "structures" included traditional societies and societies dominated by charismatic leaders. In both cases, status and honor in society determined the operation of the law. For Weber, then, bureaucracy is nothing less than the full realization of the promise of "equal protection" of the law because only bureaucracy can level the society and ensure that everyone is treated according to the rules rather than according to their status in society. It is not true, therefore, that status or honor itself had to disappear; societies could still be complex and heterogeneous. But within the jurisdiction of the law, you, as a citizen, would be treated the same as everyone else, regardless of who your parents were, how much money your family had, or if you held high office.

◇◇◇◇◇◇◇◇◇◇◇◇◇

The Thing Itself

We are always tempted to reform government agencies—to fiddle with organization charts, creating new units and scrapping old ones. We hear the sirens' song: We could do good. Things could be better. We simply need good government, good people, and sensible rules. Sure, we have problems now, but things could be good. The rules should be strong, yet flexible. Gravity should be reduced, and friction outlawed completely (I never liked it, and I think a majority of people agree with me).

Okay, the last two may seem silly, but they are no less likely than flexible rules or governments motivated by your peculiar and equally flexible conception of the good. If, as von Mises claimed, bureaucracy is the *sine qua non* of the territorially extensive state, decrying bureaucracy's rigidity is wrong-headed. We can't make government more efficient, or more like business, because it insulates officials from such pressures by design.

The thing itself, the *fundamental reliance ON the state,* is at the core of the *difficulties we have WITH the state.* Attempts to reform through reorganization will generally prove disastrous. Bureaucracy cannot be improved because its very nature is incompatible with a society of free citizens who take responsibility for their own lives and their own choices. The incentives and hierarchies in the two forms are fundamentally different.

To put it starkly, citizens may say, and believe, that the problem is unresponsive bureaucracy or corruption, but these are the essential features of the governments of large nations. The solution is a citizenry that understands the economic and political forces that make government inherently incapable of carrying out the tasks we want to assign to it. But the mainstream media, nearly entirely ignorant of basic economic principles, has no hope of aiding such an understanding and more often than not contribute to the "we can do better" mindset by carrying sensational stories of corruption inevitably followed by demands for reform.

What about the educational system? The truth is that education in economics—as opposed to trade studies in business or marketing or the applied mathematics taught as "economics" in universities—is nearly nonexistent. Therefore, citizens have a correct but inchoate intuition that something is wrong. Since they have no way of perceiving the real problem of unrealistic expectations, we reform endlessly. We spend huge resources appointing task forces and study groups and trying to get the right people in government to write the right legislation.

The U.S. has criminalized so much behavior—from eating a candy bar in a Metro station, to mild drug use, to consensual sexual practices—that our prisons are full of people innocent of any real crime. The only reason I even heard about Ms. Willett was that she is in the middle-class and an employed professional. In poor areas all over the U.S., police harass and beat nameless citizens while trying to enforce unenforceable laws. Those cops and those bureaucrats try to enforce the tax laws and the regulations on transactions and safety standards and a thousand other things. They may or may not be good people, but their failure to do good is a direct consequence of the contradictory and, in fact, impossible job they have been given: to enforce injustice.

I expect that Ms. Curry-Hagler took her tin Transit Cop badge, and herself, a little too seriously in handcuffing Ms. Willett. But the personality, the goodness (or not) of the people enforcing the law, is beside the point. We don't fall out only with the abuse. It's the state, the state itself and its logically inherent mechanisms of control and oppression, that is a hydra-headed monster of legal restrictions on liberty. The thing itself is the abuse.

Alternatives to the Thing

My claim in this book is that social problems are often made worse by legislative solutions. Such coercive solutions are inherently inflexible or tyrannical. We would be better off relying on a mix of tolerance, common sense, and private morality to deal with the fact that the world isn't quite the way we'd like it to be.

At the Munger house, for example, we snack high on the food chain. I don't know if God gave man dominion over the beasts of the field, but She certainly gave me a platinum American Express card and a big metal cart for cruising the meat aisle at Piggly Wiggly. That beats dominion.

Many of the beasts of the field, the forest, the oceans, and the air land on my stove and then my plate—sacrifices to my enjoyment. I have many friends who are vegetarians, and they have my greatest respect. They are (mostly) healthier than I am. Further, they are principled: they make a choice and they stick to it, and they don't berate me when I get a 120-ounce Porterhouse. I likewise try to cater to vegetarian tastes and make sure I only suggest restaurants with good vegetarian alternatives.

At my house, I serve vegetarian dishes to guests without even asking whether it is necessary that I do so.

This is how most big problems should be handled: locally and without resort to coercive force. We can try to persuade one another, but sometimes we should accept the fact that reasonable people can differ. That's why there is no attractive solution to the abortion debate. Our insistence on trying to solve the problem with a system of law is not just logically doomed: it is tearing communities apart. Personally, I think abortion is morally wrong and that it imposes a psychological blot that the woman can never wash away.

I also think that is my opinion, and I should keep it to myself. If you ask me, I'll tell you: Abortion is evil and harmful; don't do it. But if you don't ask, you'll never hear a peep from me, and I certainly wouldn't use the coercive powers of the state to force you or your partner to bear a child that you don't want. I think abortion is wrong, but it's also wrong for me to employ people with guns, like Cherrail Curry-Hagler, to force you to act in a way that caters to my beliefs.

Rather than try to reform the inescapably blunt and often disastrously implemented power of the state, a civilization has to realize that there are two other ways to solve the problem of actions we don't like. The first is simple tolerance, or, failing that, forbearance: putting up with disagreement and other points of view you think are wrong. That is the price of living peacefully together in a society. The other is to try to inculcate morals and manners, recognizing that the reliance on the state as the enforcer of morals and manners displaces real morals and real manners, which are voluntary.

Instead of teaching our children to be moral, and to care about social opprobrium, parents and schools abdicate their roles as shapers of minds and rely on the state to punish misbehavior after the fact. Children naturally conclude that if there is no punishment from the state, there must have been no misbehavior, but the state cannot fulfill this function for reasons of simple competence and resource constraint. Additionally, the state would fail to carry out the function correctly, even if it were competent, because power corrupts and breeds malevolence. The abuse and the thing are the same. The conviction that we can harness Leviathan is the most dangerous conceit of our age.

3. TRANSANTIAGO: When the Thing Really, Really Tries

I was sitting in the office of the Decano, or Dean, of the School of Government. I watched out the window as the sun sank into the Andes in a Dr. Seuss palette of pastels. I must have been distracted because I thought I heard the Dean say that, according to his survey results, the biggest problem facing the citizens of Santiago, Chile was...the bus system.

The bus system? Really? How could the capital of privatization-friendly Chile have botched buses?

The answer, though entertaining to an outsider, is a parable about the combustible combination of optimism and ignorance. Add a spark of "two hours late to work," and you have riots hot enough to match the sunset. Let's go over a bit of history.

Santiago's Private Buses

With more than five million residents and real economic growth averaging six percent over the last decade, Santiago is a boom town, the economic engine of Chile. Nestled in a broad basin of the Andes, Santiago has the density (21,800 people per square mile) and the wealth (banking center and headquarters to more than one hundred international corporations) to make a mass transit system work.

And work it did. The underground, or Metro, opened in 1975 and had high ridership, nearly 2.5 million daily. Like many municipal subway systems, it received government subsidies to operate, but, compared to Washington DC's fiscal black hole, "Metrorail," Santiago's was a model of efficiency. (If you are keeping score at home, the DC Metro gets annual direct subsidies of more than $175 million and average construction subsidies of nearly $1 billion per year; Santiago's Metro gets about one third that much in operating funds, and less in construction, in a metro area twice as large as metro DC.)

But the real jewel in Santiago's transit crown, or so I would have thought, was the bus system. Hundreds of different bus lines, most of them entirely privately owned, operated freely throughout the city. Some of the lines ran on surface streets parallel to the Metro, adding transport redundancy in case the Metro was having mechanical problems or was simply overcrowded. Competition among bus lines kept fares low, and drivers were paid according to the number of passengers they transported. Other bus routes delivered riders to Metro stops, not because anyone had ordered them to do so but because that is where passengers wanted to go. And there were several classes of service, ranging from posh express buses that charged high prices down to claptrap jalopies that charged pennies and stopped every few blocks.

There were two very real problems with the old Santiagueno bus system, however—as a survey of articles in *El Mercurio* and *La Segunda* newspapers in this period illustrate. Both had to do with greed or the public perception of it.

Problem one: destructive competition. Drivers were paid based on the number of passengers rather than on time or distance driven. A moment's thought reveals the problem: Take one bus stop with a crowd of passengers and then add two buses with many empty seats. The result is a 40-mile-per-hour bus race on streets full of cars and pedestrians. The drivers were taking tickets, making change, watching traffic, and reenacting the chariot race scene from "Ben Hur" all at the same time. Not surprisingly, the number of motor vehicle accidents had risen from about 10 per 100,000 population in 1990 to nearly 15 by 2005. Further, 700 pedestrians per year, nearly half of all traffic fatalities in Santiago, were killed by cars or buses, a number much higher than in many other cities in Latin America over the same period. Worse, both trends (motor vehicle accidents and accidents resulting in deaths) rose over the period 1990-2005, compared with falling rates in nearly all of Chile's neighbors. Further, there was little effective regulation of emissions, and Santiago began to suffer from uncomfortable, and sometimes dangerous, levels of smog. The bottom line was that many of the private companies operated unsafe, smoky, polluting, old hulks of diesel buses as a way of keeping costs down, and drivers competed aggressively for passengers. These were legitimate problems, and some government action was required.

Problem two: profits. This was a little hard for me to believe when first I heard it, but a major municipal mass transit system was operating *in the black*, without public subsidy. And why is that a problem? For private companies to be operating "without losses" means that the owners were going out of business (if they offered bad service) or making actual profits (if they were offering services people valued above the cost of providing the service).

But that's not the way detractors described things. For more than a few members of La Concertacion, Chile's center-left ruling government coalition, having companies profit by providing a "public service" smacked of theft. Of course, all services, including grocery stores and theaters, are "public services" of a sort, and, in fact, the Allende regime in the late 1960s and early 1970s had nationalized grocery stores and theaters for just that reason: profit is theft for those on the left.

Given these two problems, a consensus started to build. Citizens were upset about the aggressive driving and pollution, and the "planners" who run city agencies objected to having routes people seemed to want (that's what profits mean, after all). People also objected to the injustice of different levels of service with different fee structures. The planners decided that it would be better to have a comprehensive, "rational" transportation plan, one that made better use of the subway system and reduced pollution.

The result was the new "Transantiago" public bus system, rolled out on February 10, 2007, during the summer vacation period, when Santiago seems asleep. Nonetheless, almost overnight, the new "planned" system cut mass transit ridership, increased congestion everywhere in the city, and tripled average commute times from 40 minutes to two hours. As President Michelle Bachelet later said in a speech, "It is not common for a president to stand before the nation and say 'Things haven't gone well...But that is exactly what I want to say

some other way to get to work on time and avoid being fired. But this meant that traffic became impassible, as people stopped riding buses and started driving or taking taxis.

3.   The 10 companies licensed to operate by the city bought hundreds of huge, accordion-hinged "bendy buses" and put them into service on the streets. Each company operated monopoly routes prescribed by the authorities and had no latitude in level of service, frequency of service, or fares. The old competitive system, with many small and nimble buses, was entirely replaced, but the narrow lanes on many roads in the old city and mountain foothills simply could not handle the new behemoths. I have personally seen at least five wrecks where bendy buses pulled out into the middle lane to make a right turn, only to tear the front bumper off a car that had pulled forward in the right lane. A planner can't tell by looking at a map whether a route can handle a huge bus, but that's what they tried to do.

4.   Drivers were paid hourly and could be fired if they didn't keep on schedule. The old system, in which drivers were paid by number of passengers, was proudly scrapped. The new system, rather than 'rewarding greed,' was planned to improve public service. It should surprise exactly no one that this system was even worse than its predecessor. For one thing, the long hinged

buses had four doors. Of course, passengers were *supposed* to enter at the front door, and to exit through any of the rear three.

But the drivers had no reason to care about the number of paying riders, and it was very time-consuming to go back and throw non-payers off the back of a crowded 30-meter-long bus. So many drivers would simply drive their routes, operating on something close to the honor system: If you wanted to pay, you got on through the front door; otherwise, you used the rear doors. In no time, the old system where everybody paid and would hand forward their payment and get change back, hand over hand, was replaced by an "only chumps pay!" norm: a dishonor system. On some routes, at some times, less than half the passengers paid, and there was no reason for drivers to care.

Drivers did care about being on time, however. As the new routes, increased private traffic, and huge buses clogged the streets, the on-time performance of drivers deteriorated. Additionally, the drivers recognized that they didn't need to stop at all. Some drivers would simply pass large groups of passengers, some of whom had been waiting for an hour or more, even if the bus was only half-full. I have personally seen three half-full buses pass crowded bus stops. The planners had assumed that incentives only matter in the private system. In the public system, drivers worked for...the public! That may have been the dumbest assumption of all. People are people, and respond to incentives, regardless of whom they work for. Besides, these drivers didn't work for "the People"; they worked for "the State."

Any Idiot Can Criticize; What Would Work?

As I noted above, anyone can be a critic with hindsight. The question is, what *should* have been done instead? There were problems, real problems, with the old system. The buses were poorly maintained and spewed pollution. Drivers raced each other for passengers, sometimes injuring pedestrians or occupants of cars as they "overfished" what was, in effect, a common pool of possible passengers and stops. Although Chile had fewer traffic accidents than most Latin American nations, it had a rate of pedestrian injuries and deaths as high as Brazil's or Mexico's, well-known pedestrian death traps. And the streets were, indeed, congested.

A remarkable book by George Mason University Economics Professor Dan Klein and two coauthors (Adrian Moore at *Reason* and Binyam Reja at the World Bank; hereafter KMR) analyzes the problem of urban transit more deeply than any other source I have seen. KMR point out that there are two key problems with many private bus services, especially in areas where property rights may not be defined or defensible. The first is the problem of congregation, or coordinating on a stop location where a sufficient number of passengers are conveniently massed. The second problem is timing since no one makes money from a passenger waiting for a bus.

Now, monopoly public bus service "solves" the first problem by having well-defined bus stops, with (in some cases) attractive, well-lit shelters. In some locations, the road can be modified to make a pull-off lane for the bus. Public bus systems solve the second problem by having schedules.

KMR point out that there is nothing particularly "public" about either of these solutions. In fact, most public bus systems rely on government enforcement of their monopoly property right so that no private buses can pick up or drop off passengers at public bus stops. But this would work just as well for private buses, provided government simply enforces *private* rights to exclusively local pick-up areas. All that is needed for competition is enforceable "curb rights": If a bus company builds a bus stop and pays for a pull-off lane, then no other bus company can steal the passengers congregating there: different bus companies, different bus stops, and a "no poaching" enforced by government.

There are other, obvious institutional features of well-functioning private markets in the urban transit setting, and they would flourish if government regulation allowed them to. Bus companies might have two-tiered pricing systems to ensure a reliable supply of customers throughout the city. An ad hoc rider, one who simply catches a ride from one point to another without a consistent pattern (someone going across town to shop for an electronic part, perhaps) might pay a high fare. But "frequent rider" cards—which would give riders a sharply discounted fare in exchange for the promise of riding with the same bus company every day, from the same neighborhood where they live to the neighborhood where they work—would ensure a fairly stable number of regular riders.

Finally, one cannot emphasize enough the advantages of allowing competition over routes and levels of service. The argument that bad service is "fair" because literally everyone suffers places the value of equality over every other public goal, no matter how desirable. In a large, diverse urban area, some people want higher-speed express service, with amenities and, perhaps, an attendant. Others want rock-bottom prices and are willing to accept more inconvenience and less service. Charging everyone the same price and providing only one state-mandated level of service ensures that nearly everyone actually wants something else but can't get it.

The Hydra-Headed Beast

Here is the real problem with the "greed is always bad, public provision is always good" perspective. As James Buchanan pointed out in "Politics Without Romance," it makes no sense to assume that, under some circumstances (private buses), people are greedy, and, under others (government buses), people are benevolent. The fact is that people are people. In both cases, in the private sector and the public sector, people behave purposively, pursuing their own goals filtered through the incentives and costs the system presents to them. Yet, the idea persists that removing profits and using government results in a moral transformation. Many planners think that profits are evil and would prefer a system that eliminates profits, even if it means accepting substantial losses and worse service.

No matter how many times this notion is killed off by experience and evidence, the monstrous hydra of planning grows another head, and political leaders trumpet the new reform in public service. Then, when the reform fails, commissions are formed, implementation is blamed, and budgets are raised. There was an interview conducted in 2010 after the worst problems in the implementation of Transantiago were ironed out. J.C. Muñoz, a professor at Catholic University in Santiago, put it this way:

> [T]he main goal of the system was not to save time, but to reduce accidents, prevent drivers from competing for passengers, and reduce noise and pollution. **All these objectives were met from the beginning.** But the system was performing so badly that the **users could not appreciate these benefits** in the face of the poor service they were experiencing. (McConville, 2010; emphasis added)

Prof. Muñoz put his planning finger on the main problem: all they needed was more appreciative users! Those ungrateful bus riders should have realized the enormous benefits they were receiving. Sure, quite a number of them lost their jobs and had to spend an extra hour—*each way*—commuting to work, but the planners' objectives "were met at the beginning."

Of course, those objectives could also have been met by:

1. a curb rights system with private bus stops;

2. rigorous inspection and licensing with large fines for buses that fail emissions tests; and

3. allowing a diversity of routes and levels of service, thereby reducing the number of private cars being driven because the bus system sucked.

The difference is that if a private system, with reforms 1 and 2 strictly enforced but maintaining feature #3, had been implemented, the objectives would have been met while also maintaining redundancy and high service quality. Then riders would have actually been grateful because they were getting what they needed.

The Transantiago bus reforms took a badly flawed private system, operating without public subsidy and serving well over one million people a day, and "publicized" it. The expectation, almost pathetically naïve in retrospective, was that outlawing profits and demotivating drivers would change human nature. Worse, planners believed that they could dictate choices to commuters, who turned back to private automobiles instead of riding buses that followed lines drawn on maps by bureaucrats.

THE THING ITSELF

◊◊◊◊◊◊◊◊◊◊◊◊◊◊

4. CUBA: When The Thing Wins

It's May 2001, and I'm in the world's oldest army truck with three soft-looking 40-year-old "soldiers." We are outside the main airport in Havana, Cuba, but I'm in the country illegally. I didn't sneak in; I flew in on a legitimate (though tiny) commercial flight from Miami, but I didn't have a valid visa because apparently the gate agent in Miami had a twisted sense of humor. The guys in the truck couldn't have been more bored. I couldn't have been more scared, and I had never felt the absence of the 4th, 5th, and 6th Amendments as vividly as I did at that moment. I was even worrying a little about needing the 8th Amendment.

But then it became obvious that what was missing here was some money. Ten dollars, American cash. I asked in my terrible Spanish if there was perhaps an additional "fee" or tax (impuesto) that I might pay. It turned out that $30 would be enough to go back inside. As I got out of the truck to go back inside the airport, I noticed that the right front tire was flat and appeared cracked from being in the same position for months. No wonder the soldiers were bored. They had known the truck was not going to take me to a dank prison. It was just business. No hard feelings, right?

THE THING ITSELF

◇◇◇◇◇◇◇◇◇◇◇◇◇

It struck me: the Cuban system is the natural baseline, the way humans deal with each other if they are denied property and markets. Take away some misanthropic 18th century powderheads with a profound distrust of centralized power, and the U.S. would have the same system.

Remember the song, "I'd Love to Change the World"? It has a verse, "Tax the rich, feed the poor / Till there are no rich no more? / I'd love to change the world / But I don't know what to do / So I'll leave it up to you..." (If you don't remember, it is from *Ten Years After*'s 1971 album, "A Space in Time.") I had heard the song maybe a hundred times before I realized that it perfectly summarizes the view that leads to a system like Cuba, where the income distribution is fair.

If we tax the rich and feed the poor, will there be a socialist nirvana? Like the song says, "Till there are no....RICH...no more." That's all the power to tax means. You can't get rid of poor people through taxation, but you *can* get rid of the rich. Cuba got rid of all its rich people by killing them, taxing them, or scaring them to Miami.

People who are afraid of government in the U.S. often say, "Would you want restaurants run by the Post Office?" But that's the wrong analogy. The Post Office sells a product and could become efficient if it were privatized. What happened in Cuba was a hostile takeover by a *truly* abusive third world system: the District of Columbia Department of Motor Vehicles.

I'm serious. I lived in DC for a while. If you want to experience Cuba right here in the States, go to a DC DMV office and try to strike up a conversation with an employee. You will never encounter another human being who is quite that bored, or quite that angry, at everyone. There are no privileges in the line at the DC DMV. We are all treated the same: like dirt. So now you've been to Cuba. Welcome to the workers' paradise.

I had come to Cuba on an educational exchange program (I started to say "visa," but I didn't actually get one of those, as I will soon explain). A professor friend ("F") and I had been asked to give a series of lectures at the Center for the Study of the United States at the University of Havana. We had prepared stuff on the American Presidential election, and we had worked up presentations on some of the sub-cabinet appointments for Bush's government, particularly those affecting Latin America and Cuba in particular.

It quickly became clear that we were out of our league. The folks at the Center were smart, funny, and had direct outside internet access. That meant two things: first, these nice people were stone spooks—their "study" of the U.S. being simply the analytical arm of the Cuban intelligence service. Second, since they lived in a system of government where whim and personal bias was king, they knew an incredible amount about whim and personal bias. F and I wanted to talk about the American system; they wanted to know about the third deputy under-over secretary of photocopiers because they knew he was the one *really* in charge of things in the basement of the State Department.

They ended up showing us websites (these were U.S. government web sites, mind you) where you could track cabinet appointments and get detailed dossiers of potential appointees. It was clear in about two hours that the stuff I had prepared was not going to be informative, though we did all learn some things. My color overheads really impressed them, not because they don't have the technology but because they cost about $1.50 per page to produce. Figuring this was a boondoggle rather than a Duke business trip, I had gone to Kinko's and had the copies made at my own expense in Raleigh.

The reason they were impressed was that, as professors and near the top of the heap in terms of income, they were well paid—earning in some cases more than $20 per month. The idea that someone would pay nearly $30 out of his own pocket to make 18 overheads was amazing to our hosts. I later found out that many of the professor/spooks also drove taxis on nights and weekends since they could make a month's salary in tips in just a couple of days.

No Visa, No Mastercard

The U.S. requires that American citizens petition for permission to go to Cuba, and the conditions are fairly stringent. You have to qualify for an educational, artistic, or other exchange program, and the purpose has to be documented. I had done all these things with the aid of the organization sponsoring the trip, but the U.S. government is still none too pleased about people going directly to Cuba, so the airline arrangements are a bit sketchy.

In the Miami airport, I had asked four people, gotten three different sets of directions, all wrong, and failed to find the proper gate for the Havana flight in nearly two hours. When I finally arrived at the correct check-in counter, I was told that I couldn't possibly board the flight because the paperwork wouldn't go through. I took my bag down there anyway and talked to the gate agent. When I said I was there for the Cuba flight, he just laughed. "That flight leaves in 25 minutes," he said. "There is no way to get the visa forms filled out in that time."

Having lived in Texas, I was pretty confident I knew the Latino mind. Seeing the nametag on the gate guy, I wheedled, "Arturo, I am sorry for the trouble. It's just that I thought that YOU might be able to do this. But of course, now I see that it is beyond your power to get this done. I'll just get a hotel and come back tomorrow…"

Arturo's breath hissed inward, and he glared at me. "YOU…WAIT….HERE!" he half shouted. Within seconds, he had the forms and was barking orders in Spanish. Two other gate agents were recruited, and all four of us worked on forms, with me handing my passport and educational exchange visa application form around as needed. Since all the other passengers had arrived an hour early, as required by the visa system, there wasn't much else for the gate agents to do anyway.

In twenty minutes, with almost five minutes to spare, Arturo smiled and gestured to the seating area. "Dr. Munger, you are welcome to enter and sit down. Your seat number is 11A. Enjoy your flight." Feeling that my place in the world hierarchy was secure, I stepped in and pretended to read a magazine for about 30 seconds, before the flight was called and we all went out to the little "Miami Vice Drug-runner Special" prop plane that would take us the 120 miles to Havana. As Arturo took my boarding pass at the gate, he winked.

I later had a vision of the events that would transpire at Arturo's house that night. After dinner, he is helping his wife with the dishes. Arturo shakes his head, a little ruefully. "I did it again, Cipriana," he says. "I sent some jerk across without a visa."

She turns on him. "Arturo! That's so mean! You know they'll hassle him! What if he reports you?!"

Arturo laughs. "This guy was such a zangon. He'll never even figure out what happened. He obviously thought he was playing me, and he probably thinks he has some special insight into the Latino mind. I wonder how he's doing now?" Arturo looks slyly sideways at Cipriana.

She tries to look stern, but a snicker sneaks out of the side of her mouth. "SOLA VAYA!" she snorts. They both giggle, and then finish the dishes. A personal note, to Arturo: Good one, man. I deserved it.

Mastercard: You Can Leave It Home

Of course, while you need a visa to get into Cuba, you may as well leave your Mastercard on your dresser at home.

THE THING ITSELF

◇◇◇◇◇◇◇◇◇◇◇◇◇◇◇

Cubans have no problem taking plastic, but they cannot accept accounts issued by U.S. banks (that's the *U.S.* law). So Americans have to take big plugs of cash. This is really not a problem since everyone else uses American dollars also [Note: This was in 2001]. In fact, Cuba is one of the most dollarized economies in the world and has been for more than a decade. About the only thing you can buy with pesos, from the "state" stores, is dead flies and really old soap powder that has solidified into bricks.

We had quite a bit of free time for sightseeing and fun on the town, and there are plenty of things to do in Havana: Hemingway's house, touring the Morro castle, museums, parks...it's a five hundred year old city with fifty years of zealot-guano caked on top. We met three of the most interesting, sad, and hopeful people I've ever met, in three different settings. I'll describe them each briefly because each was a facet, or layer, perhaps, of Cuban society that makes the whole mixture different from anywhere else I've ever been.

One of the first things "F" and I did was to go to the Museo de la Revolucion, unsubtly sited in the former Presidential palace, last occupied by the appalling Fulgencio Batista (motto: "They voted for me before they voted against me, so the coup was justified!") on New Year's Day, 1959. Our tour guide was one of the government employees who work in the Museo—a smart, pretty, and dedicated young woman. I'll call her "Antolina."

Antolina was pretty excited about the museum/palace. She showed us the bullet holes near the stairway, where the Castro-aligned "students" had run up the stairs to try kill Batista in 1957. Batista's office was impressively ornate, and Antolina showed us the "secret" exit behind a curtain where the cowardly Batista hid from the students' righteous anger. The attack failed, she said, but it was a glorious union of the student intellectuals and the working class—the first instance of the union that still animates Cuba today—and blah, blah, blah (I'm skipping a lot).

Halfway through the tour, we went outside, to look at some displays of military hardware. I asked Antolina a question about the "students" and where they came from. Couldn't have been more innocent. She immediately turned to me and said, "Look: you two are professors. I'm an historian. Let's drop that other stuff because it's just what we tell tourists."

Then she told us her version of the real story. Remember, this was a woman who worked in the Museo de la Revolucion, as close as you can get to shrine in Cuba. She was in uniform

wanted to do…except in Cuba, where she had to spend every afternoon telling lies to tourists who paid a dollar to hear them.

The second striking personality was a semi-private, but government approved, tour guide who went with us by taxi to several sites and tried to work with us to get through an army "roadblock" that had no apparent purpose. (All the tires on their trucks were functional; I checked). He was friendly, bright, and quite energetic. I'll call him "Trino."

At lunch, F and I asked Trino about himself. It turns out he had an advanced degree, the closest equivalent one could find to an MBA in Cuba. He wanted to start his own business and had several plans about how to make it happen. We talked in general terms about what would happen when Castro finally passed on—the inevitable chaos of transition and the uncertainties afterward. I slowly realized that Trino was furious, and what made him angry was the system he had to live in (partly because that meant he had to be a tour guide to fat idiots like me!). More than anyone else I met, this tour guide made me aware of the tragedy of "modern" Cuba.

He had enormous plans—gigantic ambitions—but he had to go to Morro Castle, or Hemingway's house, or some other attraction every day and answer the same questions ("Do they have those six-toed cats here?" "No, that was Hemingway's other house—the one in Key West." (Dios, me tira ahora…)). His life was ticking by, and he couldn't organize any development ventures even though he lived in one of the largest, most attractive, and least developed tourist destinations in world. There is prime real estate right on the Malecon, one of the most beautiful ocean vistas anywhere, where the buildings are completely uninhabitable. Some visitors ask if these buildings were damaged in the Revolution. "No, ma'am. They *have been* damaged by the Revolution a little at a time, until whole blocks are dropping chunks of themselves into the street."

We had asked our spook hosts, back at the University, why these properties weren't being developed or just torn down. They earnestly explained that there were plans to renovate them but that the government had not yet authorized the money. So fixing the buildings is "complicated." I tried to argue that there was a big difference between complicated and stupid, but I didn't get very far. Yet, somehow, Miami had managed to find ways to allow private ownership to generate huge new building projects, and there was not a single building being renovated along the entire Malecon.

THE THING ITSELF

◇◇◇◇◇◇◇◇◇◇◇◇◇◇◇

But I had a job, and I was going back to my own country where the socialists are safely holed up in humanities departments in universities where they can't do much harm and only the agriculture and health care industries are nationalized. Trino had to ride by these great gold mines every day, and it was tragic. All you have to do is take ten, 26-year-old entrepreneurs like Trino, open up a financial system for direct foreign investment, and endorse private property. Within a year, each of those Trinos would be making $30k a month, the unemployment rate would drop below 3%, and the Malecon would be beautiful even if you stood with your back to the ocean instead.

The last guy was the most amusing. His type is not unique to Cuba, for his ilk can be found in any police state. The young man I'll call Evaristo was utterly charming, amusing, and completely untrustworthy, so we liked him immediately. Evaristo was selling contraband cigars in *mirabile dictu*, the government cigar shop. To be fair, he wasn't actually selling cigars there. He was trying to hook people into walking across the street (good hiding spot!) with him and buying the "same" cigars (he claimed) at less than half the price, while avoiding all those nasty taxes and laws and things.

Michael Munger

◊◊◊◊◊◊◊◊◊◊◊◊◊

Being a free market libertarian, I am completely terrified of tax dodges and black market transactions since governments have men with guns. Being a liberal, F believes in a more nuanced approach: pay the taxes you think are legit (to be fair, for F this is almost all of them) but feel free to weasel on the rest. So I paid $80 for ten cigars in the government shop, got my receipt for U.S. Customs, and followed Evaristo and F to the "private" cigar shop run by Evaristo's associates.

We got into the first floor and saw that the building was just a shell left over after a pretty severe fire. There was nothing on the first floor, including light or air (it is possible I was hyperventilating by this time). Being a coward, I stayed on the first floor while F and Evaristo went upstairs to complete their transaction. F was gone quite a while and then came down beaming. He had gotten twice as many cigars at less than half the price I paid for mine.

The cost of the Revolution, in short, is not that Cuba has failed to attract tourists. They did manage to build some hotels to house libidinous German businessmen while they wear out the local hookers. The cost of the Revolution is that it has told people they can have what they want, then told them what they

75

can actually want, and then failed to deliver even that. Don't worry; be quiet. It is not an economic system; it is a religion.

After a week, it was time to go. The taxi picked us up right at the hotel. It was a massive Mercedes, maybe two years old, and plush. It was about a twenty-five-minute ride (a little over fifteen miles) to the airport, and we swooshed along through the third-world landscape of horses pulling iron plows as if we were in a space ship. Our driver was quiet, courteous, drove just over the speed limit, stayed off the horn, stayed in his lane, and spoke passable English. In short, this was better than any taxi ride you could possibly find in Miami or New York.

When we got to the airport, the driver said, "Four-tee." F and I both heard it that way. We were delighted. This wasn't a truck with a flat tire, this was a new Mercedes, and a veteran taxi driver was ripping us off by charging us an outrageously realistic world price for a realistically high quality service—the Cuba of the future and we were the vanguard. As we tried to hand him a wad of fives and tens, the driver's eyes widened, and he shook his head wearily. Idiot Americans. "No, no: Four-TEEN."

I was tempted to tell the driver that he would still be better off with an old truck, and don't worry too much about the tires.

◇◇◇◇◇◇◇◇◇◇◇◇

Hasta La Victoria Siempre

Who cooked up this mess? It is common to blame Marx or Lenin, who came up with the original recipe, or to castigate Castro; heaven knows there are thousands of deaths and hundreds of thousands of ruined lives that Castro should have to answer for. But one of the important thinkers of the Revolucion in Cuba was its Christ-figure/poster boy, Ernesto "Che" Guevara. You won't see many images or statues of Castro (to his credit, he is personally modest in dress and lifestyle), but you will see Che everywhere, almost as much as you'll see images of Jose Martí (Imagine George Washington and Martin Luther King had a love child. That's Jose).

Guevara was what Fidel was not: handsome, brilliant, educated, a medical doctor, an accomplished writer, and (in the last years of his brief life) openly anti-Soviet. He was also capable of giving a public speech in less than five hours, a skill Castro has never developed but still works on several times a month.

For present purposes, though, there is one other important thing about "Che" (a nickname after his habit of ending sentences with the Argentinian slang for "pal" or "buddy"). Che was a *philosopher* of the revolution. To

THE THING ITSELF

◇◇◇◇◇◇◇◇◇◇◇◇◇◇

understand the "project" of revolution in Cuba, it is worth quoting Dr. Guevara at length. This is from his "Man and Socialism in Cuba" (1965). The letter attempts to distinguish the role of the individual and the collective and the project of remaking citizens.

I shall now attempt to define the individual, the actor in this strange and moving drama that is the building of socialism, in his two-fold existence as a unique being and a member of the community...

Society as a whole must become a huge school...Education takes among the masses and the new attitude that is praised tends to become habit; the mass gradually takes it over and exerts pressure on those who have still not become educated. This is the indirect way of educating the masses, as powerful as the other, structured, one.

...We can see the new man who begins to emerge in this period of the building of socialism. His image is as yet unfinished; in fact it will never be finished, since the process advances parallel to the development of new economic forms. Discounting those whose lack of education makes them tend toward the solitary road,

towards the satisfaction of their ambitions, there are others who, even within this new picture of over-all advances, tend to march in isolation from the accompanying mass. What is more important is that people become more aware every day of the need to incorporate themselves into society and of their own importance as motors of that society.

...The vanguards have their eyes on the futures and its recompenses, but the latter are not envisioned as something individual; the reward is the new society where human beings will have different characteristics: the society of communist man.

It's hard not to admire Guevara. He was an impossibly attractive combination of intellect, physical vigor, and sensitivity to suffering, besides looking terrific in that iconic Alberto Korda photo in 1960 with the beret. But he had this wrong. Dead wrong. There are no "new economic forms," and the real "motors" of a *healthy* society are people pursuing "the satisfaction of their ambitions." People "incorporating themselves into society" are people descending into a living grave.

THE THING ITSELF
◇◇◇◇◇◇◇◇◇◇◇◇◇◇◇

Cuba should be a wealthy, prosperous, and educated country. It is truly beautiful, if you don't look too closely at the collapsing buildings and chunks of concrete in the streets. The weather is great, and people run incredible "private" restaurants (paladares) out of their homes. For $18 or less, you'll get everything from appetizers to cigars, and you'll never find better camarones al mojo de ajo. The cars, rebuilt "coches de Bondo" from the mid-1950's, still run, even though not one part of the engine, brakes, or steering is original. In short, in every situation or activity where the Cuban people have been allowed to "tend toward the solitary road," they rock.

The parts of Cuba that suck are…well, everything else. The government restaurants are grossly overpriced, and the service is decidedly indifferent. The government construction projects consist of groups of men arriving to work about 10:00 a.m., staring at the walls for a while, having some lunch in the shade, and then calling it a day. Their pay almost fits this charade: less than $20 per month. But they are clearly missing their true calling. These men are ideally suited to work on U.S. DOT road projects and earn $20 per *hour*.

Now, on its face, this is not a problem. Collectivist activities everywhere are maddening wastes of time and money.

80

◇◇◇◇◇◇◇◇◇◇◇◇◇

I had no trouble recognizing the Department of Motor Vehicles service ethic, or the Department of Transportation work ethic, from my own experience here in the U.S. *The difference is that in Cuba, the messed-up collectivist part is the stuff Castro and his co-religionists are proud of.* It is just another illustration of von Mises' fundamental insight:

> *Most men endure the sacrifice of their intellect more easily than the sacrifice of their daydreams. They cannot bear that their utopias should run aground on the unalterable necessities of human existence. What they yearn for is another reality different from the one given in this world.*

THE THING ITSELF

◇◇◇◇◇◇◇◇◇◇◇◇◇◇◇

Michael Munger

◇◇◇◇◇◇◇◇◇◇◇◇◇

EDUCATION

THE THING ITSELF

◇◇◇◇◇◇◇◇◇◇◇◇◇◇◇

0

5. ATTACK OF THE CONSERVATIVE THUGS

1985, Hanover, NH: At the end of 1985, there was this utter certainty about South Africa: everyone (including I) was opposed to apartheid. But it was a protest without a disagreement. There were no pro-apartheid protesters or "PW Botha is our guy!" posters—not even any undercover apartheid sympathizers scrawling furtive graffiti.

Nonetheless, in early fall 1985, some Dartmouth students from excellent families built a "South African shanty town" to illustrate through fellowship the hardship of living in a township. The shantytown remained on the Green, Dartmouth's central quad, for months. The students evolved from indignation into sanctimony as their faculty handlers constantly congratulated them on their courageous loitering in the face of no opposition whatsoever.

October, November: the shanties were looking ratty and so were the students. This was getting boring. Sure, it was fun to sit outside in the afternoon in October, and maybe even nap in the shanty in early November. But by the middle of November—highs in the mid-30s, lows about 20°F at night—they had had enough. No one was staying in the shanties anymore, and the

THE THING ITSELF

◇◇◇◇◇◇◇◇◇◇◇◇◇◇◇

wind blew through the empty pile of broken boards and sheets of plywood.

The Dean of the College, Edward Shanahan, finally ordered the shanties removed by November 21. Since the Green was Hanover property, not Dartmouth's, the town's zoning ordinances should have been enforced. What would have happened if a *real* homeless person, one not well fed and without a warm dorm room to shelter in, had tried to build a shanty and actually live in it anywhere in Hanover? That shanty would have been torn down immediately as clearly required by the town's laws.

But Dartmouth President David McLaughlin had by this time become the Head-Weasel-in-Charge. He bravely countermanded the Dean's order, facing down the grand total of exactly zero people who favored apartheid or objected to the shantytown on substantive protest grounds. As the *NYTimes* quoted it, President McLaughlin said, "The expression of the students is not inconsistent with the expressed concerns of the college with regard to apartheid." He went on to say the shacks could stay as long as they promote "honest dialogue" about South Africa's racial policies and the school's investments. I was a little worried because that justification suggested that protests

inconsistent" with the college's own view. Is that the standard? All speech and protests are protected so long as the professors agree? Does that mean that protestors who don't have faculty support get different treatment?

Ding, ding, ding! We have a winner. Because that's exactly what happened. One of the attackers, who happened to be black, was vilified in floridly racist language and physically threatened. For all the attackers, the "charge" was some vague thing (worshipping false sledgehammers, corrupting shanties, sort of like Socrates), but the punishments were specific and harsh. On February 10, three attackers were "suspended indefinitely" (which seems a lot like "expelled"); the other nine were also suspended for either two or three terms.

The hearings were so grossly staged and mismanaged that even President McLaughlin grew two tiny little *juevos* and called for a retrial on March 5. Or maybe it was his lawyer, the "special counsel" that advised the administration that the suspendees' pending lawsuits were slam dunks because the faculty in charge of the hearings had ignored such time-honored conventions as evidence and actual appearance of witnesses. The sentences were reduced in the second hearing and later reduced again so that the worst punishments amounted to about

THE THING ITSELF

◇◇◇◇◇◇◇◇◇◇◇◇◇◇

six months suspension, and most students received no suspensions at all.

There are two persistent rumors that I want to lay to rest, because both are absurdly false. At no time did anyone set fire to the shanties, with or without occupants. The "attack" with sledgehammers consisted of three or four half-hearted blows, by which time the yells of the unexpected occupants flumoxed the attackers into backing off. The second rumor is that the attack had been planned to coincide with the MLK day observance. I asked about this one myself because I was incredulous: it couldn't be coincidence. But the *DR* kids told me, and I fully believe them, that they had specifically *waited until after midnight*, so that it was Tuesday January 21, and therefore *technically* no longer MLK day, before carrying out their covert mission.

So the attackers were guilty of being idiots. The symbolism of sledgehammers in the night, right after the first MLK day observance, and with people actually *in the shanties*, reveals a political ineptness so deep it wouldn't be seen again until Republicans thought they could win favor by shutting down the government.

But still, no university can say that some protests are sanctioned, or even endlessly subsidized, while other points of view are punished just because the administration happens to agree with one view and not the other. Either protests are allowed on the Green or they aren't. This was a protest; this was the Green. The *DR* students should have been reprimanded for vandalism. The person who actually swung the hammer should have been charged with the mildest type of assault, and that should have been the end of it. I'm not even sure about the assault part because I really believe the "attackers" didn't know there were any occupants, since the shanties had usually been empty for more than month.

Instead, across the country, the attack by "conservatives" galvanized the shanty movement. Soon, there were shanties on every flat space on college campuses. The good news is that more than a few colleges did divest, and, even more important good news, F.W. de Klerk released Nelson Mandela and the African National Congress held legal organizational meetings in South Africa in 1990.

But Mandela's release and the organizational meeting in 1990 didn't happen because of divestment or because of shanties. Diversting was fine because it meant that U.S. colleges and the firms they invest in were not morally complicit in apartheid. But the actual cause of the collapse of Botha, de Klerk, and the South African "boys in the hoods" was the collapse of communism, and the bravery of black (and some white) protesters in South Africa itself. The divestment movement may have been a feel-good thing (though it seemed to me more like a feel-cold thing), but its actual impact was negligible. Apartheid was terrible, but that horror didn't justify, or really have anything to do with, the desire of a small minority of American university faculty and their student allies to repress anyone who raised questions about the "movement."

A couple of brief postscripts:

1. On March 13, 1986, a group of seventeen Dartmouth students were convicted of having resisted the final removal of the shanties, effected on February 11 with hydraulic hammers (the plywood floor was under ice, inches deep in places). One of those students pled guilty to *intentional physical assault on a police officer*. No administrative actions or punishments of any kind were handed down by Dartmouth.

2. On October 16, 2000, the *Manchester Union Leader* did a "where are they now?" (Rose, 2000) article on the three

ring-leaders, DR editors Frank Reichel, Deborah Stone, and Theresa Polenz (Admit it, you thought all three key figures were men, didn't you! Are you more surprised that women swing sledgehammers or that women can be conservative?). According to the *MUL*, Reichel noted, with hindsight: "It could have been done in a more politically palatable manner—it could have been done in a little softer—but that's not the way the Review has operated...It was not meant as a violent act; it was not meant as an aggressive act against any one person; it was not meant as a political act; it was meant to preserve the green....If there's trash in the public street, you can pick it up."

THE THING ITSELF

◇◇◇◇◇◇◇◇◇◇◇◇◇◇◇

◇◇◇◇◇◇◇◇◇◇◇◇◇

6. POLITICAL CORRECTNESS AND THE ACADEMY

August 1986: I was 27-years-old and two years out of grad school. We were trying to balance Wheat-Thins and cheese cubes on plastic plates and holding our plastic glasses filled with bad Chardonnay. The "New Faculty: Welcome to Texas!" party had been going on for nearly half an hour, but it was quiet as a tomb. What do you say when there's nothing to say? Then the Dean, a grouchy-looking man in a nice suit, walked out to an open space among the fifty or so newcomers. Incredibly, he took a plastic fork and thuk-thuk-thuked it against his plastic cup, making no sound and spilling wine. But in the silence he soon had our attention.

"Now, I want you all to listen to me, because this is important." He smiled, as if about to say something clever. "I don't want to hear about 'teaching, how much teaching' you are all doing. You are here to do research." He gave a big smile now, avuncular, in a Slobodan Milosevic way. "This is a simple business: you will be judged on how much research you produce. You have to teach, you *all* have to teach, but I don't want to hear anything about it. You have to teach well enough that I don't get any complaints. But..." (here his voice rose:

97

louder, higher) "…you will be judged solely on your research records when it comes to salary, retention, and promotion decisions!" His words echoed for several seconds. "Are there any questions?"

There weren't any. He had been pretty clear—psychotic, but clear. I expected him to shriek, "If you doint eat yer meat, ya canna have any pudding! How ken ya have any pudding, if yer woint eat yer meat?" Welcome to the large American university.

The University of Texas has more residents than most counties. In fact, UT would be (according to the U.S. Census Bureau for 1986) the 825th biggest county in the U.S. (that's out of 3,141), bigger than Henry County, VA, but smaller than #824 Stanly County, NC. Folks tell you "everything's bigger in Texas!" but you would have to see the UT campus to believe it. I went to a small liberal arts school—Davidson College, near Charlotte, NC. It had (when I was there in the 1970s) about 1,100 students. At UT, I team taught *one class* ("American Government and Texas Politics") that at 1,200 students had more bodies than all of Davidson, *every semester*. The overall undergraduate population hovers between 45,000 and 46,000, with another 10,000-plus graduate students. The UT website trumpets, "UT is the nation's largest university."

Then, the entryway signs for the Texas Memorial Museum on campus trumpet that the statue of the "Texas Pterosaur" is the "largest flying creature ever discovered on earth!" It is common for a Texan to tell you, proudly: "We're bigger than France!" Texans will ask you, "What is the biggest one-state highway?" You might think it's the I-10, from Orange to El Paso, but that's only 879 miles. The winner is U.S. 83—903 miles from Brownsville to the Panhandle's tip. And that is big: 900 miles is the distance from Boston to Myrtle Beach, passing through ten states along the way. Still, what is the deal? Why does everyone in Texas talk so big?

There are hints that something deeper is going on. The first is the water and the terms Texans use to describe it. Don't look for lakes; there aren't any. The thing that Texans call a "lake" is a dammed-up river. Now, what they call "rivers" are gullies with standing water. "Creeks" are gullies without standing water—just dust. And "gullies" are your backyard, at least in the Hill Country around Austin. Fifty years or so ago, life in the Hill Country was tough and not very graceful. Why would Texans want to pretend that it is paradise?

The answer is not complicated: Texans assume, plausibly, that outsiders (particularly Yankee academic outsiders) will look down on them, so the natives bluster and brag and look out of the corner of their eyes to see if the professors are impressed. They are not impressed, of course, for a reason equally uncomplicated. Most faculty, particularly in the social sciences and humanities, are politically leftist. Now, don't get me wrong—leftists love "The People." Of course, fleas love dogs, so maybe I'm over-interpreting. I do think it is fair to say that the academic left is most comfortable thinking of "the People" as an abstraction that needs the assistance of academics to arrange the basic outlines of life. It's much harder to deal with the People one by one, as actual people. The idea of engaging with a nonacademic—someone not aware of the self-evident genius of Foucault, FDR, and Derrida—is very upsetting to your average humanist scholar.

It took me about a week, New Hampshire/Dartmouth transplant that I was, to take the Texan's side on this point. My wife and I never lived in the burbclaves of academics north of the University; we chose instead to live south of Town Lake (which is, of course, not a lake but just the dammed Colorado River). People at the University would ask us, "How can you live with...Texans?" and then laugh as if they had said something clever. For many young academics, Austin was a

Chekhov play made real. They lived impossibly far from Moscow but desperately aped the manners of the Muscovite (okay, Cambridge, New Haven, or Palo Alto) elite. If only they could do as the grouchy Dean commanded, they might even publish their way out of exile, and all would be well. In the meantime, they could dream, read their Sunday New York Times, and study the job openings back in the civilized world.

The distain of my colleagues for Texan students was remarkable. The hallway talk would have been funny, except that these faculty were quite serious. "I can't believe how conservative everyone is," they would whine. "Do they not have any good teachers in the high schools?" The solution was obviously "education," but my colleagues thought of education the way Pol Pot thought of it—a remaking, by force if necessary. For many of the instructors in the humanities and social science departments, the supposed subject of the class was of little importance. These "teachers" saw their purpose in life as forcing students to confront the fact they are hypocrites and racists.

Political Correctness: A Shibboleth

Without reprieve, adjudged to death,

For want of well pronouncing shibboleth.

–John Milton, "Samson Agonistes"

THE THING ITSELF

◇◇◇◇◇◇◇◇◇◇◇◇◇◇

It has become unfashionable to use "politically correct" approvingly, but it was not always that way. Today, PC is always used mockingly, either by conservatives who sneer that the "PC movement" has taken over universities, or by liberals who use the phrase to make opponents sound petty or shallow. But the first time I heard the phrase, it was uttered with utter approval by a liberal colleague. He agreed with something I said, noting that, "It sounds like it would work, and it's also *politically correct*."

As for so many other topics, the best insights I have seen on this subject come from F.A. Hayek, in this case from his 1973 book *Law, Legislation, and Liberty*. He describes the beliefs that most people adopt, and then persist in:

> *That human institutions will serve human purposes only if they have been deliberately designed for these purposes, often also that the fact of an institution exists is evidence of its having been created for a purpose, and always that we should so redesign society and its institutions that all our actions will be wholly guided by known purposes.* **To most people these propositions seem almost self-evident and to constitute an attitude**

alone worthy of a thinking being. (pp. 8-9, emphasis added)

What are they so sure of? What view does the left take that has come, as Hayek rightly notes, "to constitute an attitude alone worthy of a thinking being"? It is that markets and independent thought may, at best, be a necessary evil? Real freedom requires planning and control, though the whom behind that planning and control is not clear, since the very people who are too dumb or selfish to think for themselves will now have to think for others. Mannheim famously states this view:

> *At the highest stage freedom can only exist when it is secured by planning. It cannot consist in restricting the powers of the planner, but in a conception of planning which guarantees the existence of essential forms of freedom through the plan itself. For every restriction imposed by limited authorities would destroy the unity of the plan, so that society would regress to the former stage of competition and mutual control.* (p. 378)

The very idea of "political correctness," then, is the product of two linked certainties: a goal and a process. The first (goal) certainty is the moral superiority of planned economies and centralized hierarchy of manufacturing and education systems with equality of *outcome* and the absence of opportunity for social differentiation through effort or excellence. The second (process) certainty is the inevitability of historical "progress" toward this goal as societies evolve and improve. Together, these two certainties constitute a dynamic teleology, with both moral and historical force. This is the essence of progressivism.

To be politically correct, then, is not simply to pay lip service to current fads of speech or fashion, such as what name to call a minority group to avoid insulting its most sensitive members. Political correctness is the sense that there is an approved, acceptable account of history, and that people who disagree are evil, delaying progress, and misleading the gullible masses.

But in 1988 I didn't understand any of that. That's why, the first time I heard someone use the phrase "politically correct" I burst out laughing. I was standing at a water fountain in Burdine Hall, home of the Government Department on the University of Texas-Austin campus. A colleague who didn't know me very well, and who certainly would never have suspected me of the heresy of political incorrectness, stopped to chat. He mentioned that Jesse Jackson (who was running for

President, and to whose campaign my colleague had contributed a small sum) was going to be giving a speech that night.

I assumed he would be excited about the speech. This same colleague had been mentioning Rev. Jackson for weeks, and when he told me about the speech, I mentioned that I assumed he would be glued to the TV. "Oh, no," said my colleague. "I really don't like to listen to him. He doesn't have many concrete policy proposals."

I was amazed. "Why are you supporting him if you don't think he is a good candidate?" I asked.

He was surprised I didn't understand. He spoke slowly, as you would to a child. "Well, given how corrupt and unjust the American democratic system is, the choices we make don't matter anyway, so you might as well be politically correct."

What he meant, of course, was that you should pick the candidate who most visibly serves the agenda of the left, purely as a symbol (in this case, by being African-American). Since there is no possible objective substance, or meaning, to democratic politics (he assured me that Michel Foucault had proved this), we should all make *symbolic* choices that serve the good. To do otherwise, particularly if you actually believed in one of the candidates, was to be duped by shadowy people who

105

"control" the process. In short, the sign of his depth and cleverness was precisely the absurd superficiality of his choice criterion.

Over the next couple of years, I heard the phrase "politically correct" fairly often, and without exception, it came from the mouths of people with leftist views who claimed not to believe in objective truth. In fact, the assertion that some things were simply correct—and that they knew it because truth is actually self-evident—and acting on this knowledge quickly became an important shibboleth.

(Aside: I'm always surprised how few people know the story from *Judges* 12, verse 6. "Shibboleth," meaning an ear of corn, or a flooding freshet or stream, was a word that the Gileadites could pronounce correctly but which the Ephraimites, lacking the "sh" sound, pronounced "sibboleth." This makes me wonder, how did the Ephraimites tell people to be quiet in theaters or the library?)

But the left's use of "politically correct" as a pass phrase didn't last long, though of course the underlying certainty about truth persists. Before long, in fact, the abbreviation to "PC" had become an even more powerful shibboleth for the political *right*. If you said you favored hiring a woman, or African-American, you might be accused of "caving in to the PC movement," even if you genuinely thought that the candidate was simply the best person for the job. This is the meaning of PC that is most common today, and it's just as worthless as the original meaning.

In fact, no person on the left would dream of using the phrase, except derisively. I have been asked, and I think the questioner was serious, "What are you doing, becoming PC all of a sudden?" The incident occurred when I spoke out in favor of a minority candidate for admission to a graduate program. The questioner, knowing I was skeptical of affirmative action, pressed me hard about my motive for saying we should admit the candidate. "She's got great GRE scores, good letters, and solid grades," I said.

"Yes, but she's Native American," came the reply. "I know you conservatives don't like minorities; why are you going all PC on us all of a sudden? What are you up to?" I started to say that I neither favored nor opposed minority candidates as minorities but wanted to look at their qualifications as individual people, but I quickly realized that trying to make this argument was missing completely the basis of the idea of political correctness.

THE THING ITSELF

◇◇◇◇◇◇◇◇◇◇◇◇◇◇

PC-ers think that there *are no* standards; there are only symbols and politics. In fact, the very concept of "standards" is a code word for "racist." So while the use of "politically correct" has changed dramatically, the meaning hasn't changed at all. If there are no standards, no objective means to judge, then conformity with a subjective political doctrine is the only metric.

7. RED-BAITING BAITING

I am Called a Red-Baiter

"I have here in my hand a list of two hundred and five [people] that were known to the Secretary of State as being members of the Communist Party and who nevertheless are still working and shaping the policy of the State Department."

–Senator Joseph R. McCarthy, speech, Wheeling, West Virginia, February 9, 1950

"Red-baiting" is a political tactic, one that demagogues on the right—especially, but not only, Senator McCarthy—used in the 1940s, the 1950s, and in some ways continue to use. It is reprehensible because it plays on the fears and sense of patriotism of otherwise good people, duping them into serving some purpose of demagogues. For the person called a "Red," the result in the 1950s could be devastating: loss of job, denial of future employment, even physical threats.

It is tempting to think that was then, and this is now. Things have changed, right? But people on the left really do still have some legitimate fears. We no longer think of a backlash against leftists as "red-baiting," of course, since outside of

THE THING ITSELF

◇◇◇◇◇◇◇◇◇◇◇◇◇◇

English and literature departments (and people who ought to be in those departments but don't know it) there are no more Marxists. Without a worldwide movement and the sinister muscle of the Soviet Union, it is hard to say why people are so worked up when someone on the left expresses his or her views.

But they do: questions about U.S. foreign policy, whether in Latin America, Africa, or more recently in Afghanistan and Iraq, bring angry reactions. Instead of addressing the issues, demagogues on the right have questioned the patriotism of dissenters, and accused them of aiding America's enemies. This is illogical (disagreeing with U.S. policy hardly implies that you support the policies of our enemies), but it is rhetorically useful. It puts the dissenter on the defensive, and instead of considering aspects of U.S. policy, the "debate" turns to an examination of attitudes of the dissenters themselves. "My son is a boy scout! I own an American flag (though I don't fly it, because that's jingoistic). I pick up trash on the jogging trail! I drive a Volvo, but it has American-made tires! I *love* America!" After you have been called a Red, or a traitor, a few times you (as Bruce Springsteen put it) "end up like a dog that's been beat too much, 'til you spend half your life just coverin' up."

◇◇◇◇◇◇◇◇◇◇◇◇◇

Here's the thing: you might think that people who justly fear academic and intellectual repression would be less likely to practice it. You would be wrong. One common repressive tactic of the academic left (I won't talk about the academic right, or unicorns, or other non-existent creatures) is to transform a question about policy into cause for accusation about attitude. A common tactic is to label anyone who disagrees with your views a "racist." Since racist is such a powerful accusation, and since racism actually is a real and present force in American society, it is a knockout blow and ends the debate. After you have been called racist a few times, you stop arguing and just smile when someone says something stupid.

But the cruelest tool of the academic establishment dates from the 1980s. It is "red-baiting baiting." That is, you accuse someone of red-baiting when all they have done is try to argue with you. The fact that this is silly has not limited its use in the context of the academic establishment of the last thirty years in the least. Consider an analogy: the reason that "racist" is so effective as an accusation is that there really are very few African-Americans in positions of power. In fact, there aren't many blacks in positions of *anything* in universities. Many times, I have been in large meetings with one or two black

111

faculty at most. If a statement in that setting is labeled racist, I might wish that the accuser would be more careful, but it is at least not logically absurd on its face that blacks really are an underrepresented and excluded minority in academics.

But red-baiting? C'mon! Most of the time at a dinner or a meeting I am the only person who falls outside of the "left to far-left" range. What in the world do you think would happen if I were to label a faculty member an extreme leftist? As far as I can tell, it means that person would get an endowed chair and go on to write prose so chuckleheaded that s/he would win the "Turgid N. Opaque" award. Being called a leftist is either a compliment or a commonplace. You might as well call someone a "biped."

In the spring of 1989, there had been a series of complaints from students about the fact that professors in the University of Texas government department were "too liberal." In my opinion, the problem was simply that the professors were too lazy to teach, so they spent class literally shouting at students about how ignorant the students were. "Hey, you, orange shirt in the fourth row. Do you know that the government of El Salvador is a fascist puppet of the U.S. imperialist plutocracy? I bet you don't because you are a defender of patriarchy!" (That, by the way, is a nearly verbatim quote. You could hear these performances from the classroom next door, where I was trying to talk about the *Federalist Papers*). Now, the choices for answers to these questions were "yes" or "no," and neither one was much help in terms of learning.

Still, as far as I was concerned, even these surly and unhelpful rantings were clearly protected under the umbrella of academic freedom, at least in any one classroom. If some West Texas kid from Burkburnett or Floydada comes to Austin and doesn't get to see some "fahr-eatin' liberals," he ought to ask for his money back. Part of our job as faculty is to take people out of their comfort zone. Further, there was no evidence, at any time, that political views had an effect on the grades given to students. The complaints had been of the piecemeal, "we don't like this professor" form rather than any organized protest based on one incident that clearly crossed a line of propriety.

Notice that I said "in any one classroom." What I meant was that if academic freedom protects the liberals, it has to protect the conservatives. Academic freedom doesn't mean you are free from criticism; it means specifically that you must be protected from job-related reprisals (firings, salary cuts, or denials of raises or promotions) by the administration. It cannot *possibly* mean that you are protected from other faculty expressing their own, possibly opposing, views. The person who said this best, in my experience, is Barry Saunders of the Raleigh *News and Observer*: "Freedom of speech means you can say what you want, but then you still got to take the ass-whuppin'." The right to say what you want, and the right of others to criticize you, are the *same right*, folks.

Academic administrators are disproportionately (on the order of ten to one, or more) relatively liberal. Bleating about being oppressed within the university for expressing liberal views is absurd. At Texas, at least in those days, the only thing you *absolutely* had to do was avoid creating complaints about your teaching. If students complained about a faculty member being too liberal, or anything else, that faculty member needed to make some changes. The point is that, even though the "go forth, and create no complaints" standard appears content-neutral, it might very well have the effect of restricting academic freedom of speech.

The Department decided to take strong action: it formed a committee. It apparently wasn't taking the problem very seriously, though, because the chairman asked me to be on the committee. As a third-year junior person, I had little knowledge and even less power, but it was my first administrative committee assignment, and I was determined to do my best.

The agenda of our first meeting was clear: decide how to deal with the complaints that a few students had verbally leveled, for no single incident and probably for no good reason, against two of the instructors in the government department. All the complaints, and there hadn't been that many (less than ten total, in two classes of sixty or seventy each), were something vague about the professors being "too liberal." This seemed pretty easy to me: we needed to say that these were normal complaints because there was no evidence of grading bias or misuse of power and no real bulling. In short, there was no action that justified interference with the classroom teaching of these faculty.

When it came time for the meeting, though, I was shocked. The committee chair said that there was good news: The department had done a great job of dealing with the complaints of previous years. This year, there had been, in fact, no complaints at all.

Gosh, that doesn't seem right. After all, there *had* been complaints, but the complaints were not anything actionable. I wanted the department to take a stand and defend academic freedom, not tell lies and pretend that no one had complained. In retrospect, I came across as pretty obnoxious and was probably just wrong. The distinction between "no complaints" and "some complaints but nothing important or specific" was not nearly as earth shaking as I was pedantically making it out to be. Still, I could not have predicted what happened next.

The head of the committee was furious. "What sort of complaints?"

I knew the answer to that: "Some of the students have complained that the instructors are 'too liberal' and that they make the students uncomfortable. Now, I think…"

He interrupted me: "Have there been complaints that *you* are *too conservative?*"

I later realized that he thought he was threatening me, but I wasn't clever enough to understand. This should show you, though, that the very idea that professors might be afraid for being liberal, inside the administration, is far-fetched. Most committee chairs and most mid-level administrators lean left. The others have toppled over on their left sides entirely. But what I said next, in my ignorance, made things worse. "Suppose there *have* been complaints, *about me*, about being too conservative. Then there *still* have been complaints, and our committee needs to address them. You said 'there have been no complaints,' and that's not true, even if the complaints are about me. Your question proves that we can't say there have been no complaints."

He got very quiet then. He asked me what the complaints were, though of course he knew. We had discussed them in the hallway. Then he asked me, quite formally, what classes the complaints had been addressed to. This was again unnecessary because that is why the committee was formed in the first place, but I played along and named the courses and the instructors. Then he closed his notebook, looked at the other two committee members, who had not said a word, and announced that the meeting was now over.

This seemed like a funny way to run things, but okay. I went home. When I came in the next morning, I walked by the open door of one of the instructors whose class had been the subject of the student whining. The person howled at me, "So! You don't like my class? Why didn't you have the courage to come tell me yourself instead of stabbing me in the back?"

I actually was so dumb I didn't know what the person meant. "No, I don't have a problem with your class. What do you…"

THE THING ITSELF

◇◇◇◇◇◇◇◇◇◇◇◇◇◇◇

"You made a formal complaint yesterday to the administration! You said I was too liberal. How dare you?"

What the committee chair had done, of course, was scuttle down the stairs to the main office and say that *I*, Michael Munger, was the one complaining about the class. The difference between, "Munger says there have been complaints (and they are unjustified)," and, "Munger is complaining about your class," is a pretty big misrepresentation. Another word would be "lie." The committee chair had told a bald-faced lie.

I tried to explain, but the instructor I had "ratted" on was beyond wanting to hear explanation. This person had thought we were at least casual friends, and here I had complained about the person's class in a "secret" meeting (question: how secret can it be if the committee chair runs around reporting what people said in the meeting or, in this case, making up things that weren't even said in the meeting?).

Heading back into the hallway, I heard a booming voice. "Doing a little red-baiting, are you Munger?" The speaker was a friend, a guy way on the left-side of the political world but a perfectly decent and thoughtful fellow. We had been over to each other's houses and went to lunch at least twice a week. I tried to explain to him what had happened, but he had already made up his mind. "Munger, this is why we can't have conservatives in the department. When it comes down to it, you people can't help yourselves. You have to play the commie card!" I could see that he was laughing at me and half-joking.

But he was also half-serious. The academic left needs to see itself as being outré, oppressed, and the "other" in the society in which it lives. If the left started to think of itself as conventional and established, two things would happen: First, they would actually be responsible for the problems and inadequacies of American university education, rather than the rebels trying to make things better against overwhelming odds. The second is that many people on the left (not all, maybe not even most, but many) require a sense of "otherness" to be able to survive psychologically. Intellectual laziness and moral bankruptcy are not very attractive; much better to see yourself as beaten down and discriminated against by "the man."

I had to give up, and I did. I apologized to the two instructors whom I had "wronged." Let me say, if I had complained about their courses, either to their faces or behind their backs, it *would* have been wrong. Given what they knew, they had every reason to be upset. I wish they had let me explain, but they had done nothing blameworthy. The committee chair was a different matter. The amazing thing was that, by the time I talked to him again, he had convinced himself that his distorted account (that I had complained, rather than there had been complaints and I wanted that to be known) was true. He took me to lunch and tried to have an avuncular talk, saying that I needed to curb my ideological extremism.

I was in no position to argue, though I was in a position to leave, and did so as soon as I could get an outside offer. In August of 1990, I left for the University of North Carolina at Chapel Hill, taking a pay cut of nearly ten-percent just to escape.

Concluding Remarks

There are two final statements I want to offer. First, the atmosphere and outlook of the administration at the University of Texas have changed markedly since I left in 1990. Though there are still several departments with questionable leadership, by and large, the University has turned substantially in its attitudes toward students and made marked improvements in the intellectual life of the campus. Although it is still enormous, and some kids lose their way in such a gigantic setting, it is possible to get a first-rate education at the University.

Second, I don't want to attribute evil motives to anyone in my story. The paranoia and self-conscious "otherness" of the left is part and parcel of the secular religion that has grown up in the establishment of the academy since the 1970s. What strikes me as strange is the ability of the academic left to accept the contradictions in their own position without questioning themselves. It is true, of course, that this may be the essence of intellectualism. F. Scott Fitzgerald famously said, "The test of a first-rate intelligence is the ability to hold two opposed ideas in the mind at the same time, and still retain the ability to function." But what the left does is something different: they don't hold two opposed ideas at the same time; they take two opposed ideas and make them one by denying the other.

In 1988, many of my colleagues at Texas were big fans of the Democratic candidates. At first, most were loudly in love with Jesse Jackson and then in the final campaign became Michael Dukakis worshippers. Their reasons were mostly that the Democratic candidates were "for the people," and it was of "the people" (not themselves because they were unselfish and giving leftists) that my colleagues were always thinking.

The day after the election, I came into the department whistling (I was pretty happy because I had voted for the winner, George H. W. Bush). Okay, I was singing, which was pretty obnoxious: "Happy days are here again; The skies above are clear again; So let's sing a song of cheer again; Happy days are here again!"

One of my colleagues, standing at the water fountain, yelled out: "Oh, screw you!" Fair enough. I was singing; I deserved that. In fact, the person was smiling, so this was just the sort of "my team lost, so bite me!" reaction I expected and would have given back if the situation had been reversed. But as I got closer, I saw that there were tears in the person's eyes and the smile was more of a rictus of hate.

"I don't know of one person, not one, who voted for that idiot Bush except you. How does that make you feel to be the only one? Doesn't that make you wonder if you have it all wrong?"

This seemed odd, to say the least. Bush had won the Electoral College by 426-111: a pretty handy victory. The popular vote was closer, of course, but Bush had still won by nearly 7 million votes. That is, out of 89 million or so votes, Bush had secured 48 million.

Furthermore, in Texas itself, the place where we all lived, 56% of the voters had trudged into the booth and cast their ballot for Bush. That's nearly 3 million people in Texas alone that my colleague had never met or even heard of. The great mass of people who worked at jobs, paid taxes, sent their kids to school, and made political choices based on their own best judgment were completely unknown to my colleague. And this person was proud of that, considering it a badge of honor not to know or even to have to rub shoulders with any of those nasty people who actually worked for a living. Not surprisingly, this person was also one of those who lived in a secluded Yankee enclave of wannabes yearning for returning to the northeast and the folkways of their Chekhovian Moscow-wannabes.

How can one love "the people" and yet hate the very individuals who make up "the people?" The answer can be found in one of my favorite jokes, one that sums up most of what can be understood about the left in the academy. It goes like this: A fire-breathing liberal is standing on soapbox on a street corner regaling the crowd about how their lives will be better after the Revolution. "Come the Revolution, things will be better! Come the Revolution, there will be no property, and you will have everything you want! Come the Revolution, you will all eat milk and honey three times a day!"

In the back, a timid fellow said something, but the speaker couldn't hear it. The speaker roared, "*What*? What did you say?"

THE THING ITSELF

◇◇◇◇◇◇◇◇◇◇◇◇◇◇

The timid guy raised his voice. "I said, what if I don't like milk and honey?"

The speaker is outraged and glares at the questioner. "Oh, my friend, that's easy. Come the Revolution, you *will* like milk and honey!"

With only a few exceptions, the academic left doesn't like people at all. They have generally never talked to anyone who doesn't fully share their views. The series of educational and employment choices that lead to a career in the humanities or social sciences nearly guarantee a kind of isolation and groupthink that is self-perpetuating.

I guess it comes down to this: Reasonable people can disagree about the best form of government and the nature of the good society. If you really don't know anyone who disagrees with you, you shouldn't take that as a sign that you are right. It means you should get out more, and try to find a place that serves something besides just milk and honey. You might like it.

8. HIRING, ACADEMIC FREEDOM, AND DIVERSITY

In 2004, there was a substantial and, in my opinion, quite useful debate at Duke University about the role of "diversity" in faculty population and in education. The "Duke Conservative Union," a student group, had published an open letter to the President, Dr. Nannerl Keohane. The DCU noted that the ratio of Democratic registration (142) to Republican registration (8) among faculty and administrators indicated a lack of "diversity." A forum was held on March 1 to discuss the open letter and the larger issues it raised.

An article was published about the forum in *Duke Magazine*, June 1, 2004. The article, "Debating Party Parity in Faculty Population," is worth excerpting as an introduction:

> *Controversy erupted after the Duke Conservative Union (DCU) published a full-page "open letter" to Duke President Nannerl O. Keohane as a paid advertisement in* The Chronicle *on February 9. The advertisement reported a disparity in the political affiliations of university administrators and faculty members, offering a breakdown of the number of Democrats and Republicans who teach in each department. An*

overwhelming number of faculty members are Democrats, according to the group, and this, the DCU argued, was evidence of Duke's lack of intellectual diversity.

Robert Brandon, chair of the philosophy department, told The Chronicle that "we try to hire the best, smartest people available...If, as John Stuart Mill said, stupid people are generally conservative, then there are lots of conservatives we will never hire. Mill's analysis may go some way towards explaining the power of the Republican party in our society and the relative scarcity of Republicans in academia. Players in the NBA tend to be taller than average. There is a good reason for this. Members of academia tend to be a bit smarter than average. There is a good reason for this, too."

...In a Chronicle letter to the editor on February 12, Keohane acknowledged that the DCU "raised a question that deserves a thoughtful answer...For me, the question is not the personal political views of members of our faculty or their party affiliation, it's the quality of their scholarship and the strength of their teaching, which

includes ensuring that classrooms are open to diverse, often contrary, views."

...Keohane added that she believes that "no single political perspective has a monopoly on intelligence" and that classrooms are impoverished if they "become sterile forums where only bland views can be expressed and everyone is overly careful not to offend. Clear statements of well-articulated, provocative views stimulate deeper thought, and more discussion, than the cautious expression of ideas designed not to make anyone uncomfortable."

...In response to the controversy, the Provost's Office, along with Duke Democrats and Duke College Republicans, held, on March 1, a panel, "The Politics of Academic Freedom: Does Political Affiliation Matter?" Playing to an almost packed auditorium, five panelists from different disciplines and across the political spectrum weighed in on academic freedom, what makes a good professor, and whether or not there are hiring biases at Duke when it comes to political affiliation.

THE THING ITSELF

◇◇◇◇◇◇◇◇◇◇◇◇◇◇

What follows is a verbatim transcript of the speech I gave as part of the forum, but a few words at the outset seem appropriate. First, the fact that I was a department chair and by this time had won two teaching awards was a sign that I was hardly "oppressed" because of my political views. Second, though almost everyone in the crowded auditorium disagreed with me, I was heard respectfully, or at least without interruption, throughout the entire speech. Third, the issues here are complex and have more to do with pedagogy than with some score-keeping mentality of "diversity." At a minimum, it is important to keep in mind that the answer to leftist bias in hiring, if such a thing even exists, cannot be a palliative rightist bias in hiring. It's the same offense. Two wrongs do not make an educational environment.

Here is the speech transcript:

****

I think it's pretty clear what my role is here. Let me say that I'm going to argue a position that's rather more strong, I guess I'll say, than my own beliefs for the sake of having a vigorous discussion and if you get mad at me: "Good."

What we've done so far reminds me of an old joke. There's a prosecutor questioning his star witness and the witness is just giving devastating testimony. You see, the witness saw the defendant in the Circle K with a gun, holding it up. The defense attorney panics and he leaps to his feet and he says, "Your honor, I object! I can easily call to the stand dozens of witnesses who did not see my client do that holdup!"

Well, that kind of testimony would not be relevant, but folks, that's all we have heard here tonight. Professor Van Alstyne: he didn't see the holdup. Now his discussion, I think, was useful background about the AAUP, but we're talking about undergraduate students in the College of Arts and Sciences. Professor Van Alstyne, for perfectly good reasons, isn't in the College of Arts and Sciences. He never teaches undergraduates. Now, imagine that a faculty member wanted to berate a conservative student for her views. Has anyone claimed that such a faculty member would say, "Wait, we've got to get an appointment with Bill so I can go over to the Law School and berate you in front of him"? I expect not. Ditto more so for Mr. Adcock. Has anyone alleged that our faculty specifically traveled to Mr. Adcock's office to berate undergraduates in front of the university counsel? He's Duke's defender. He defended Duke. If we had a highway patrolman and asked him about speeding, he'd tell us that speeding is against policy and then he

129

himself would probably speed on the way home. Most of us would. What can we infer from the incidence of speeding from the fact that speeding is against policy? Nothing. It's an empirical question. The point is that the policy is routinely violated. He wasn't in the same county as the holdup; how could he have seen it?

Now Dean Schlesinger might have seen the holdup in principle. He teaches some undergrads. He's in the College of Arts and Sciences, but his presentation here addressed the Appointments, Promotions, and Tenures Committee. Now let's see a show of hands, we can do a survey. How many people came here believing the following argument: the all-Democrat departments have fought for offers to conservative candidates only to have those offers rejected by APT?

Here's a true statement: every conservative faculty member recommended for by the literature department has been tenured. That's also true of every unicorn and every talking dog, so it's a vacuously true statement. Now, how is this setting here different from my joke where the devastating eyewitness is balanced by non-witnesses who did not see the crime even though it happened? Well, there are a couple of differences.

First, in this case, the devastating eyewitness is going next to last, and secondly...well, no, that's actually the only difference.

When I first arrived at Duke, there was a party for new faculty, and when it was time to sit down, we were all told: "Since you've been hired at Duke, I'm sure that none of you is so foolish as to be conservative. So, please, spread yourselves liberally around the tables." Now, I wasn't offended. I wasn't worried. I would never have mentioned the incident except I recently heard several people who were at that dinner and who laughed at that joke loudly insisting that politics should never play a role in hiring. If one can be certain—spread yourselves liberally—that the hiring process results in the process of hiring liberals only, how can one claim that ideology has no role in the hiring process?

Now, I don't see that a litany of incidents where I heard similar comments made by administration officials in an off-hand or joking way serves any purpose. I hope that you will stipulate this, that you will just accept it as a fact, so that I don't have to bore you for quite a few minutes with that sort of thing. Let me emphasize, it's always unofficial; it's not a statement of policy, I don't think that there is any policy that takes that effect.

THE THING ITSELF

◇◇◇◇◇◇◇◇◇◇◇◇◇◇◇

It's just an expectation. The policy is for openness. The actual expectation is that we'll generally hire liberals.

Let's take a step back. The answer that we've heard repeatedly since the publication of a party affiliation list by the DCU is that smart people aren't conservative. What was meant, of course, in fairness to the benighted Robert Brandon, is that educated people are statistically disproportionately liberal. Let's concede that. As education goes up, people are more likely to be liberal. I've often myself worked as an expert witness in legal cases involving allegations of discrimination based on the federal civil rights statutes. Now, I've usually worked for the organization defining itself against the charge, but I can use the usual method for investigating the pattern of disparate treatment of some protected class. Let me say—I think it's important—conservatives are not and should not be a protected class. There's no way I think anyone can try to make an argument that conservatives deserve status as a protected class. We're not discriminated against. But let's suppose that, just for the sake of argument, there is any possible evidence here of a pattern of disparate hiring practices given the data.

As you recall, the history department has the distinction of having 35 registered Democrats and zero registered

132

Republicans. The defense that we've heard offered is that not many people who hold a PhD in history are Republicans. Let's suppose that's true. Let's suppose it's 90 percent. Let's suppose that 90 percent of history PhDs are Democrats and only 10 percent are Republicans. Now we'll define the event of hiring a Republican as having a probability of one in 10 for each of 35 independent Bernoulli trials. How likely is it if we use the binomial distribution to proportion the discipline are 90 percent Democrat? How likely is it that a department would have zero Republicans? If the hiring process is ideology blind, the answer is .025. That's less than three chances in 100. So if, in fact, it's an ideology-blind process and it's 90 percent—90 percent—disproportionately more Democrat, 35 times is only going to get you three chances in 100 that that's an ideology-blind process.

Well, it may come down to qualifications, and here is the nub of the problem, and then I'll close. Many conservatives in many fields in the humanities and social sciences are unqualified because they are conservative as it was condescendingly explained to me just the other day. I'm quoting this. It was a remarkable incident, but I am quoting. "Asking history to hire a conservative is exactly like asking biology to hire a Creationist—someone who denies evolution."

THE THING ITSELF
◇◇◇◇◇◇◇◇◇◇◇◇◇◇

Being conservative is by definition not intellectually respectable. Conservatives are simply not qualified. That was not an administrator—that was no person in a position to put that into effect—but I think it's a widely shared view. So the claim that most of the qualified applicants are Democrats or even more liberal than Democrats is probably true. It would explain why most faculty in the social sciences and humanities departments are not conservative, but it would not in itself explain why there are no Republicans. The problem is not too many Democrats; the problem is too few Republicans to be able to say it is an ideology-blind process. There is no other explanation for the overwhelming disparity.

This is not a legal problem. There's no justifiable claim; it simply isn't true that conservatives have suffered historical discrimination in society. There's no justifiable claim here. I think it's perfectly fair to ask as a matter of educational policy whether a total lack of conservative voices is consistent with our goals as a university. It may be, but it's not obvious. It would have to be argued. I haven't heard an argument yet, only some defenses against charges that no one has made from witnesses who didn't see anything. Thank you.

✳✳

Michael Munger

◇◇◇◇◇◇◇◇◇◇◇◇◇

In the time that has passed since this forum, I have heard from quite a few people about the argument I tried to make in this speech. There's not much I would need to change if I were to give it again today—partly because the ratio of party registration at Duke, and in the academy generally, hasn't become any more balanced. On the other hand, I want to emphasize something I said in the speech: I don't think we need to have affirmative action for conservatives. What we need is faculty who are committed to education rather than ideology.

THE THING ITSELF

◇◇◇◇◇◇◇◇◇◇◇◇◇◇◇

9. COLLISION WITH ERROR: Our Education System is Failing the Left

A much-loved professor at Duke, Dr. James Bonk, supposedly gave a make-up test to four young men.

The young men were said to be confident they would do well on his chemistry final, so they took a road trip to UVA and stayed out too late drinking. There was a problem with the alarm, and they ended up missing the exam completely.

They begged the professor to give them a make-up exam, as they "had a flat tire." The story goes that Prof. Bonk gave them the exam the next day with all of the four young men sequestered in separate rooms.

- The first question, worth five points, was simple: the molarity of a solution.

- On the second page, worth 95 points, was an essay question: "Which tire?"

We laugh at the discomfiture of the students caught in this all-or-nothing trap. But in, at least, some cases, our students face a similar kind of test—one based not on facts but on ideology. The one-question test is this: "Are you a liberal or conservative?" And the correct answer is, "I'm a liberal and proud of it." That concerns me.

137

THE THING ITSELF

◇◇◇◇◇◇◇◇◇◇◇◇◇◇

However, the nature of my concern may surprise you. I'm not worried much about the folks who get it wrong; for the most part, they actually get a pretty good education. There are relatively few instances of clear bias in grading or treatment, other than being mocked or made fun of. But in ten years, I only had one serious complaint about a grade based on political bias. That student had received an A-. An A-!

No, I'm worried about the folks who get it right. Our educational system is failing *the students on the left*. They aren't being challenged, and they don't learn to think. Students on the left, rather than the right, ought to sue our universities for breach of contract. We promise to educate them, and then all we do is pat them on the head for memorizing the "correct" answer!

I was the Chair of Political Science at Duke for ten years. After about two years at a meeting of department heads, we heard from the chair of one our Departments of Indignation Studies.

(I should explain that we have several departments named "Something-or-Other Studies." In most cases, these departments are really constituted for the purpose of focusing indignation about the plight of the Something-or-Other—a group that has suffered real and imagined slights and now needs an academic department to be indignant in. Some of the scholars and teachers in our various Departments of Indignation Studies are excellent researchers and gifted teachers, but the conception of Indignation Studies itself is not one I much admire. We will likely gather these departments together into a School of Indignation Studies at some point and get some large federal grants.)

Anyway, at the meeting of administrators, the chair of one Department of Indignation Studies looked around and then said, "I probably shouldn't say this, but I find that I don't really need to spend much time with the liberal students because they already have it right. I spend most of my time arguing with the conservative students. That's how I spend my time in class."

I found myself agreeing with her. She probably should NOT have said that.

But maybe not for the reason you think; this woman was teaching conservative students how to argue, how to think about arguments and evidence, and how to make arguments in a way that's brief and persuasive. She was educating the conservative students.

The liberal students? They were given a one-question test. Instead of "Which tire?" they are asked, in effect, "Are you a liberal?" If the answer is yes, then they seem to be told that they already "know what they need to know."

It may have come as a shock to the parents of these liberal students that they had learned everything they needed to know...*in high school*! The professors feel that these good students can be left alone and needn't be pestered with reading or learning. Having memorized a list of correct arguments, a kind of secular leftist catechism, they were free to wander around the quads of Duke and enjoy themselves.

I certainly don't mean to single out Duke. In many ways, Duke is the least politically correct and most intellectually open place I've ever worked. Compared to University of North Carolina, University of Texas, and Dartmouth, Duke makes a real effort to teach students to think rather than recite. In some ways, the students who are attracted to one of the Departments of Indignation Studies had already decided what they thought and what they want to think long before coming to Duke. And, fortunately, a number of these departments are now scrambling for students. Enrollments are falling as students choose science, information technology, medicine, or economics and public policy.

So that's the real message I want to deliver. Once we realize that the problem with our educational system is that we are short-changing the students on the left, denying an education to kids just because they happen to agree with the professor, then we actually have a way to move forward. Let me explain. The way I think of this comes (as many truths come!) from John Stuart Mill.

Mill argued that we should think of education and our overall approach to education as collision with error:

> *...the peculiar evil of silencing the expression of an opinion is, that it is robbing the human race; posterity as well as the existing generation; those who dissent from the opinion, still more than those who hold it. If the opinion is right, they are deprived of the opportunity of exchanging error for truth: if wrong, they lose, what is almost as great a benefit, the clearer perception and livelier impression of truth, produced by its collision with error.*

So the absence, in many departments, of dissenting voices is harmful—not so much harmful to those who would agree with the dissenting voice but to those who are denied the chance to collide with error. Let me continue quoting Mill:

THE THING ITSELF

◇◇◇◇◇◇◇◇◇◇◇◇◇◇◇

There is the greatest difference between presuming an opinion to be true, because, with every opportunity for contesting it, it has not been refuted, and assuming its truth for the purpose of not permitting its refutation. Complete liberty of contradicting and disproving our opinion, is the very condition which justifies us in assuming its truth for purposes of action...

If the cultivation of the understanding consists in one thing more than in another, it is surely in learning the grounds of one's own opinions. Whatever people believe, on subjects on which it is of the first importance to believe rightly, they ought to be able to defend against at least the common objections.

It's as if we are asking students to play chess, but then we only teach them one-move openings. They think that pawn to king four is a better move than pawn to king's rook four, but this is simply a matter of faith. All their lives, they bleat, "Pawn to King Four!" when asked and receive praise and perhaps a treat: "Good liberal! Here, have a cookie!"

Conservative students, by contrast, actually learn to play chess. They study the whole game, not just the first move. They learn countermoves; they consider the advantages of different approaches; they search out empirical arguments; and they read articles and white papers, perhaps like those published by the John William Pope Center, which does such a great job in providing that sort of material to those who care enough to look.

Mill summarizes the difference brilliantly:

> **He who knows only his own side of the case, knows little of that.** *...if he is equally unable to refute the reasons on the opposite side; if he does not so much as know what they are, he has no ground for preferring either opinion.* (emphasis added)

What happens when a leftist student happens to confront arguments he or she disagrees with? After all, they do sometimes hear views that contradict their own. The problem is that they have always been rewarded for one-move chess games. They think the game is over, and their opponent—if wise or virtuous—will simply concede. Anyone who continues to disagree is of course either not wise or not virtuous.

In fact, there is a ceremony that goes along with this—something one of my colleagues calls "The Women's Studies Nod." When someone makes a ridiculously extreme, empirically unfounded, but ideologically correct argument, everyone else must nod vigorously. As you nod, crinkle up your eyes and have

143

THE THING ITSELF

◇◇◇◇◇◇◇◇◇◇◇◇◇◇◇

your chin tremble for a moment, nearly cracking with the emotions of affirmation welling up from your soul. Not just, "Yes, that's correct," but "Yes, you are correct; you are one of us; we are one spirit and one great collective shared mind."

What if someone withholds the Nod? What if they frown and then make their own chess moves, raising counterclaims? Since the children of the left have never actually had to play a full chess game of argument, they need a response. And the responses are two: "You are an idiot; no one important believes that," or "You are evil; no good person could possibly believe that."

Interestingly, it is at this point that the left faculty teach the left students many different moves. Let's consider a few, which you may or may not have heard of. Suppose I claim that rent control is a primary reason why there is such a shortage of affordable housing in New York City and San Francisco. Here are the responses I have gotten from students:

1. Micro-aggression!
2. Check your privilege! (Snap fingers in the face, then turn around. If they had a mic, they'd drop it because this is supposed to be so devastating.)

3. You must take money from Satan...or Koch Foundation (a franchising arrangement?).

4. Economists don't understand the real world.

5. Prices don't measure values. Values are about people. You don't care about people.

I could go on, but I won't. Notice that not one of those responses actually responds to, or even tries to understand, the argument that rent control harms the very populations that politicians claim they are trying to help. The point is that if you cared about poor people, actually cared about consequences for poor people, you would oppose rent controls. Paul Krugman opposes rent controls; Robert Reich opposes rent controls.

But that's not how the logic of the left works. Instead of caring about the poor, they want to be *seen* as caring about the poor. That leads them to the style of argument that I laid out back at the beginning of this book: There is a problem because some people are not as well off as we can imagine they might be. We must do something. X is something. We must do X. If you say X is a bad idea, you must hate the people we care about. And if X does not succeed, the answer is...more X! We didn't do it enough.

THE THING ITSELF

◊◊◊◊◊◊◊◊◊◊◊◊◊◊◊

Of course, our colleagues on the left could choose to educate students on the left, but if you accept my claim that education actually requires "collision with error," then that is no longer possible. The faculty on the left were themselves educated by neglect—never confronting counterarguments—in a now self-perpetuating cycle of ignorance and ideological bigotry. There are some leftist faculty who learn from conservative students, but since they generally dismiss those claims as ignorant or evil, faculty can't learn much that way.

One person who famously tried to "educate" other faculty was a hero of mine, Milton Friedman, who won the Nobel Prize in 1976. What might Prof. Friedman have thought of the problem I raise? He might justly have claimed that I am wrong because he had, almost by himself, educated thousands of leftists—at least those who were willing to listen. But he probably wouldn't say that because he was modest about those kinds of achievements.

It's more likely that he would have said that the answer is competition and empowering consumers to make their own best choices. The problem is that education is a difficult arena for this argument because students don't know what they don't know, so it's hard for them to know what they should want to know.

Nonetheless, it is in the direction of competition that our best hope lies. Let me make briefly an argument for why a consumer-driven revolution in education will change, and in some ways has already changed, the dominance of the left in the academy.

To start with, this is a consumer-driven business in spite of what college faculty think. There is no other industry that blames failure on its customers. Not even General Motors claimed that car-buyers were too stupid to appreciate their genius. But that is what many traditional colleges have been doing: Our students fail, we don't. We're great!

Students see through that. Many students, even those on the left, perhaps especially those on the left, recognize that they are being patronized rather than educated. Here are some examples from my own experience:

Example 1: *The Rental*: At one of the prestigious Ivy League institutions of the northeast, there is something I call the "Rent a Conservative" program. Practically speaking, there are no faculty outside of the range "Liberal Democrat" to "Overt Communist." To be fair, I'm a fan of Marxist theory, and think it should be taught. Heck, I teach big parts of Marx's writings; he was the first Public Choice theorist. So I do believe that "diversity" includes people who disagree with me. But that's because I believe in diversity of ideas. If whole swaths of ideological perspectives are just unrepresented, not present…that's not diversity, and it's not education.

Well to their credit, sort of, this university brings in outsiders to give lectures. They aren't really willing to take a chance on tainting themselves with actual faculty positions, but the students do get a chance to hear lectures. After one lecture—and I should say that this was on a Friday night, at 7:00 p.m., prime drinking time for college students—before nearly 120 students, some members of the audience crowded up around me. One young man waited until the others had left. He shook my hand, and I could see that tears were welling up in his eyes. "I…I want to thank you," he said. "I've never talked to a smart person I disagreed with before. I'm going to have to spend the rest of the weekend doing research to figure out why you are wrong. I'm going to learn something, and I'm grateful." Now, of course, tears were welling up in my eyes.

I don't see my job as converting students; they can decide on their own. But I do want students to figure out better reasons for what they think they believe. This young man actually saw a four or five move chess opening for the first time and was thrilled. How can you get better if you don't play against good players?

Example 2: *Reproductive Rights*:

A friend of mine at Duke, a fellow who is surprisingly curmudgeonly for a young guy, also happens to have views that are pretty far left politically. But he is more concerned about education than indoctrination, and so sometimes it's hard to pin him down. He was giving a lecture on "reproductive rights," and the subject of abortion was part of it.

He asked the students, "What are the best arguments against unlimited, publicly subsidized abortion?" There was silence. The students just stared at him. Arguments *against* abortion? But…how could that be? As I mentioned, my friend is a bit curmudgeonly, and so he was annoyed at the silence. "Okay, listen. Here are three pretty good arguments against having abortions be unlimited, available even in late term, and publicly subsidized." I won't give the arguments here because that's not the point.

The point is that one young lady in the front row burst into tears. He asked her what was wrong. She said, "It's not fair of you to say those things. I have no idea why those arguments are wrong; in fact, they sound right. That's not fair!"

Now, my friend happens to be pretty extreme in his personal defense of reproductive rights. He thought that all three of those arguments had solid rebuttals, and ultimately were unpersuasive, but that was because he knew the arguments against abortion, had thought about them, and could come to a conclusion. He could play out the whole sequence of logic and evidence, move by move. Most importantly, he had presented the arguments fairly and in detail. Teaching isn't about telling students *what* to think but rather helping them learn *how* to think.

Now, I disagree with many university faculty on our conclusions about policy and ideology, but I find that I prefer a fair-minded disagreement to bland, superficial agreement. Students certainly learn more from having their beliefs challenged. Let me share part of an article from the Duke *Chronicle*, an article written by student Andrew Kragie:

> *Sept 24, 2013: "Have I Changed?"*
>
> *I went to my econ class taught by Michael Munger...who preaches free market economics like born-again Baptists preach Jesus' salvation. I found myself listening attentively as he explained that profits come from*

voluntary exchanges that improve the welfare of both buyer and seller. So profits are a good thing: Trade benefits both parties and naturally produces profits as a byproduct, even if they're shared unevenly. My do-gooder...self of two years ago would never have entertained the thought that profits could be good—after all, they all go to evil corporations. He praised [Wal-Mart] for doing business more efficiently than small firms and, thus, allowing people, especially poor people, to get more things they want and need... I felt perturbed that I couldn't field a decent argument about the chain's negative impacts. Am I drifting from my liberal roots?

Education, when it works, pulls up your roots, but it also helps you begin to grow new ones—deeper ones. After many of my classes, my students tell me, ruefully: "I used to know what I thought. Now I'm confused." Great! Because it's actually not true that you "thought" before. You just felt. The bottom line is that a young person's mind, once stretched by a new idea, never shrinks back to its original dimension.

In Closing

Two points are relevant here.

THE THING ITSELF

◇◇◇◇◇◇◇◇◇◇◇◇◇◇◇

1. Many students want more and suspect that there is more. They want to hear the best argument from the other side. It's more interesting to play against the first team. Conservative students are already challenged. We might wish that things were a bit different, but by and large, a committed conservative student comes out of a place like Duke with a real education.

2. Many faculty also know there is more to education than what is done in many classes and many majors. Many people on the left actually care about education. We have allies we don't use and friends we don't recognize. The issue is not ideology; the issue is commitment to education. And places like Hillsdale for undergraduate work or George Mason for grad school may in some ways make things worse.

I sometimes hear a rather insulting caricature: A racist is someone who is winning an argument with a minority person. A sexist is someone winning an argument with a woman. A truer version is that a soon-to-be-sad husband is someone who thinks he is winning an argument with his wife.

Those are insulting because they don't credit the arguments of the other side. Sometimes, people really are racist or sexist. It's a mistake to overuse those accusations, though, precisely because they do happen, and we should save the accusation for instances where attitudes, not arguments, are at the heart of the matter.

Here's the thing, though, the real heart of the matter. We have to convince our colleagues on the left of this truth—and many of them believe it already: The real racism is to assume that a person of color is not capable of playing the full chess game of argumentation. The real sexism is to assume that women can't understand complex arguments and have to settle for bromides and memorized "correct" political dogma.

Education requires collision with error, and if our sides make arguments respectfully, intellectually, and insist on balance first in our own classrooms, then we can change education in this country. At worst, we can be the catalyst for making the children of the left confront the problems with their own arguments.

This means we have to persuade. I shudder when I see people on our side who want to solve the problem of political correctness simply by reversing the polarity. Conservatives who don't understand liberal arguments are just as brain dead as the worst graduates produced by our most craven Departments of

THE THING ITSELF

◇◇◇◇◇◇◇◇◇◇◇◇◇◇

Indignation Studies now. If you don't learn what you stand for and why, you'll fall for anything. I hope that American education can stop its fall and once again become a light to the world.

Michael Munger

◇◇◇◇◇◇◇◇◇◇◇◇◇

CONCLUSION

THE THING ITSELF

◇◇◇◇◇◇◇◇◇◇◇◇◇◇

10. DEMOCRACY IS A *MEANS*, NOT AN END

Everyone loves democracy. Ask an American if there is a better form of government, and they'll be insulted. You believe in democracy, don't you? And what exactly is it that you believe in? What people mean by "democracy" is some vague combination of good government, protection of individual rights, extremely broad political participation, and widely shared economic prosperity. One might as well throw in an ideal body mass index and a great latke recipe. It's all good but doesn't mean much, and few people like to think about what democracy really means.

It is fine to celebrate the great achievements of democracies once they are firmly established. But such celebrations confuse cause and effect. The reason democratic nations have personal liberties, property rights, and rule of law is not that they are democracies. Rather, nations that have those things embody the entire package of the Western tradition of good government. Requiring that government actions hinge on the consent of the governed is the ribbon that holds that bundle together, but it is not the bundle itself. Fareed Zakaria identified this "bundle" problem perfectly:

THE THING ITSELF

◇◇◇◇◇◇◇◇◇◇◇◇◇◇

> *For people in the West, democracy means "liberal democracy": a political system marked not only by free and fair elections but also by the rule of law, a separation of powers, and the protection of basic liberties of speech, assembly, religion, and property.* **But this bundle of freedoms—what might be termed "constitutional liberalism"—has nothing intrinsically to do with democracy and the two have not always gone together, even in the West.** *After all, Adolf Hitler became chancellor of Germany via free elections.* (*The Future of Freedom*, p. 17, emphasis added)

So...just what is democracy? In our mental potpourri, good government leads the list. But then what is "good government?" A starting point could be voting and majority rule: most people can choose for all of us, and majorities can impose their will on minorities.

Such blanket endorsements of majority rule make me wonder whether democracy is a fraud or just a conceit. As William Riker pointed out in his 1982 book, *Liberalism Against Populism*, the claim that "fair" processes always, or even often, lead to "good" outcomes ignores much of what is known about institutions and institutional change. If people disagree, and if there are several choices, democracy is manipulable, even dictatorial. For modern political science, this is called the "Arrow Problem," after Kenneth Arrow.

If democracy is a civil myth, a conceit, it could be useful. The idea of democracy honors common people, calming the mind and pleasing the agora. If democracy is a fraud, however, then we are in bleaker and more sinister terrain. The pretense that in the multitude we find rectitude is dangerous: many of us would love to impose our "wisdom" on others. Saluting the collective wisdom is simply a way to hold other citizens down whilst we steal their purses or pack their children off to war.

And it has ever been thus, as Polybius tells us:

The Athenian [democracy] is always in the position of a ship without a commander. In such a ship, if fear of the enemy, or the occurrence of a storm induce the crew to be of one mind and to obey the helmsman, everything goes well; but if they recover from this fear, and begin to treat their officers with contempt, and to quarrel with each other because they are no longer all of one mind,—one party wishing to continue the voyage, and the other urging the steersman to bring the ship to anchor; some letting out the sheets, and others hauling them in, and

> *ordering the sails to be furled,—their discord and*
> *quarrels make a sorry show to lookers on; and the*
> *position of affairs is full of risk to those on board*
> *engaged on the same voyage; and the result has often*
> *been that, after escaping the dangers of the widest seas,*
> *and the most violent storms, they wreck their ship in*
> *harbour and close to shore.* (Polybius, *Histories*, Book
> VI, Chapter 44, ca. 130 B.C.E. (Translated by Evelyn S.
> Shuckburgh, 1889))

This is not a call for dictatorship, however. The core of the
Arrow problem is that societies choose *between* two evils: the
tyranny of a Hitler or the potential for incoherence described by
Polybius. My thesis is that "democracy" without the safeguards
of constitutional liberalism is *both* tyrannical *and* incoherent—
the worst system imaginable.

The U.S. is Not a Democracy

None of this was news to the American founders.
Elections helped citizens control elected officials and little more.
This early skepticism is plain, as in this passage from Federalist
#10:

> *...a pure democracy, by which I mean a society*
> *consisting of a small number of citizens, who assemble*

and administer the government in person, can admit of no cure for the mischiefs of faction. A common passion or interest will, in almost every case, be felt by a majority of the whole; a communication and concert result from the form of government itself; and there is nothing to check the inducements to sacrifice the weaker party or an obnoxious individual. Hence it is that such democracies have ever been spectacles of turbulence and contention; have ever been found incompatible with personal security or the rights of property; and have in general been as short in their lives as they have been violent in their deaths. Theoretic politicians, who have patronized this species of government, have erroneously supposed that by reducing mankind to a perfect equality in their political rights, they would, at the same time, be perfectly equalized and assimilated in their possessions, their opinions, and their passions.

America is a federal republic, with horizontal separation of powers among executive, legislature, and judiciary, and vertical separation of powers between the central government and the states. The Declaration of Independence is straightforward: the American system is based on the claim that all citizens have rights, and "That to secure these Rights, Governments are instituted among Men, deriving their just Powers from the Consent of the Governed..." That means that elections are still important. We need elections, literally *depend* on them, to make the whole system work. But elections are not the ends of government but the means by which citizens can withhold consent.

The problem is that the rules, procedures, and the basic "machinery" of electoral choice *as a means* have not kept up with the faith people seem to have in democracy *as an end*. We try to divine the will of the people, their "intent," on complex questions. Who can forget Florida in 2000, where officials held ballots over their heads, trying to see light through partially detached bits of cardstock chads?

Elections cannot work this way—not in a nation four times zones wide (not even counting Alaska or Hawaii). Though we demand instant information in other aspects of our lives, electoral fairness requires that the states withhold information until all the polls are closed. Voting precincts must sacrifice efficiency (which new paperless voting technologies would appear to offer) for legitimacy (where paper receipts are available and where recounts involve actual physical checks of ballots, one by one).

But you knew about this problem, which is mostly technical. I am trying to argue that there is a different problem that is at least as important: *we don't just demand too little of our democratic procedures; we are expecting too much of our democratic process.* The educational system in the U.S. has failed students because we don't know limits of unlimited democratic choice. We teach that consensus is a value in itself, even though we know that true consensus appears only in dictatorships or narrowly defined decisions. As James Buchanan, Kenneth Arrow, and a host of public choice scholars have shown, *groups cannot be thought to have preferences in the same way that individuals do.* To put it another way, it is perfectly possible, and legitimate, for reasonable people to disagree. The role of democracy is not to banish disagreement but rather to prevent political disagreements from devolving into armed conflict.

But then, in what sense does government depend on "the consent of the governed?" The American system seems cumbersome, but it combines the notion of a republic (where policy choice is indirect) with separation of powers of legislation (where an overlapping consensus is required). A majority of the population is required to pass the House, but a majority in a majority of the states is required to pass the Senate. Then the President, whose constituency is the entire nation, must separately consent before the bill becomes law. The result is far removed from "democracy," but the system does ensure the fundamental democratic principle: government can't do things to us unless we, the governed, give our consent. Elections are a check on tyranny, not a conjuring of the will of the people.

Where Do We Go From Here?

Policy makers must understand the twin anachronisms that complicate the failures of voting institutions and democratic ideologies in the U.S. There really are two distinct anachronisms, each of which requires immediate attention.

First, our technology of democracy is too old and prone to abuse or at least distrust. We must bring voting technology into the 21st century because we accept much less than is possible. We must immediately solve the problem of guaranteeing mechanisms for recording and counting votes that are beyond reproach. As the election of 2004 shows, we are nearly out of time.

Second, our ideology of democracy, our notion of what democracy can accomplish, is anachronistic also. But in this case, the anachronism is not out of the past but out of a utopian science fiction future; therefore, we must also take voting ideology *back* to the 19th century where it belongs. We have come to expect much more than is possible from democracy and democratic institutions.

This essay may make me sound like an enemy of democracy—some kind of elitist nut. Well, that's not entirely wrong. But describing democracy's flaws is not the same as arguing the virtues of elitism or dictatorship. I just want to foster humble skepticism about what democracy really is and what it can actually accomplish. Many policy conflicts hinge on whether the public can tell individuals what to do. There is a subtlety that is often missed in policy debate: there is a difference between *public* decisions and *collective* decisions. Public decisions affect everyone because they affect others besides ourselves: we can only have one defense budget; polluting rivers befouls my water and yours.

Collective decisions, on the other hand, affect everyone because the majority is empowered to force its will on everyone. There need be no true public aspects to the decision as a policy outcome; we have just chosen to take the decision out of individuals' hands and put the power in the hands of the mob.

THE THING ITSELF

◊◊◊◊◊◊◊◊◊◊◊◊◊◊

Now, it may very well be the case that many collective decisions are also public. But we need to see the line dividing private and collective choices and defend it fiercely. As P.J. O'Rourke notes, the fact that a majority likes something doesn't mean that the majority should get to choose that something for everyone:

> Now, majority rule is a precious, sacred thing worth dying for. But—like other precious, sacred things, such as the home and the family—it's not only worth dying for; it can make you wish you were dead. Imagine if all of life were determined by majority rule. Every meal would be a pizza. Every pair of pants, even those in a Brooks Brothers suit, would be stone-washed denim. Celebrity diets and exercise books would be the only thing on the shelves at the library. And—since women are a majority of the population, we'd all be married to Mel Gibson. (O'Rourke, *Parliament of Whores*, 1991, p. 5).

The real key to freedom is to secure people from tyranny by the majority, or freedom *from* democracy. The problem, then, is what Fareed Zakaria called "illiberal democracy." The metaphor we use to understand ourselves matters because it figures in how we try to advise others:

> *For much of modern history, what characterized governments in Europe and North America, and differentiated them from those around the world, was not democracy but constitutional liberalism. The "Western model of government" is best symbolized not by the mass plebiscite but the impartial judge.* (Fareed Zakaria, *The Future of Freedom*, p. 20)

The framers of the U.S. Constitution fully recognized that there is nothing, *nothing at all*, inherent in democracy that ensures the freedom of persons or property. When we advise other nations about how to devise better systems of government, our own historical skepticism about the power of pure democracy can be neglected only at our peril. When we offer advice to a developing nation, we need to advocate something like the U.S. model. Thomas Hobbes said, "Covenants, without the Sword, are but words." The modern equivalent might be this: "Democracy, without the Bill of Rights, is but tyranny."

THE THING ITSELF

◇◇◇◇◇◇◇◇◇◇◇◇◇◇◇

SOURCES

Adler, Eric. 2001. "What Fresh Hell is This?" *Women's Quarterly.* Spring.
http://www.findarticles.com/cf_dls/m0IUK/2001_Spring/75453031/p1/article.jhtml

Bastiat, Frederic (1995) *Selected Essays on Political Economy.* Irvington-on-Hudson: Foundation for Economic Education.

Bible Gateway, King James 21st Century Version, http://bible.gospelcom.net/

Burke, Edmund, *A Vindication of Natural Society: or, a View of the Miseries and Evils arising to Mankind from every Species of Artifical Society. In a Letter to Lord ** by a Late Noble Writer,* ed. Frank N. Pagano (Indianapolis: Liberty Fund, Inc., 1982). 2/3/2015. http://oll.libertyfund.org/titles/850

Caldwell, Bruce. 1997. "Hayek and Socialism." *Journal of Economic Literature.* 35: 1856-1890.

Chekhov, Anton. 1993. *The Three Sisters.* Dover Thrift Edition.

D'Souza, Dinesh, "Shanty Raids at Dartmouth: How a College Prank Became an Ideological War," *Policy Review.* Hoover Institution. 1986.

Federalist Papers. 1961. Edited by C. Rossiter. New York: New American Library, 558.

THE THING ITSELF

◇◇◇◇◇◇◇◇◇◇◇◇◇◇

Guevera, Che. 1965/2009. *Socialism and Man in Cuba.*
    Boston: Pathfinder Press; 3rd edition

Hart, Jeffrey, "Freedman and the Review: A History,"
    Department of English, Dartmouth College,
    http://69.57.157.207/about.php

Hayek, F. A. 1973. *Law, Legislation, and Liberty: A New
    Statement of the Liberal Principles of Justice and
    Political Economy.* Chicago: University of Chicago
    Press.

Hayek, F. A. 1988. *The Fatal Conceit: The Errors of
    Socialism.* Edited by W. W. Bartley, III. Chicago:
    University of Chicago Press.

"Head of Dartmouth says that Shanties are a Proper Protest,"
    The New York Times, November 24, 1985, Late City
    Final Edition, Section I-67.

Humboldt, Wilhelm von. 1993. (English edition, translated by
    J. W. Burrow), *The Limits of State Action.*
    Indianapolis: Liberty Fund.

Juvenal, Decius Junius. 1999. (Edited by Peter Green).
    Juvenal: Sixteen Satires. Penguin Classics.

Klein, Daniel, Adrian Moore, and Binyam Reja. (1997). *Curb
    Rights: A Foundation for Free Enterprise in Urban
    Transit.* Washington, D.C.: Brookings Institution.

Kragie, Andrew. 2013. "Have I Changed?" *Duke Chronicle.*
    September 24.

http://www.dukechronicle.com/articles/2013/09/24/hav
e-i-changed#.VNoLmS5aQpA

Mannheim, Karl. 1940. *Man and Society in an Age of
Reconstruction: Studies in Modern Social Structure*.
London: Kegan Paul.

McCarthy, Joseph. 1950. "205 Speech." Speech on February
9 before the Ohio County Women's Republican Club in
Wheeling, West Virginia. *History of the Bureau of
Diplomatic Security of the United States Department of
State*,
http://www.state.gov/documents/organization/176702.p
df

McConville, Megan. 2010. "Q&A: Three Years of
Transantiago." *The City Fix*, March 26.
http://thecityfix.com/blog/qa-three-years-of-
transantiago/

Mill, John Stuart. 2002 (1859). *On Liberty*. Dover Thrift
Edition.

Milton, John. N.D. (ca. 1670) *Samson Agonistes*. Edited by
John Churton Collins. Archive.Org,
http://archive.org/stream/samsonagonistese00miltuoft/
samsonagonistese00miltuoft_djvu.txt

Mises, Ludwig von. 2013. *Epistemological Problems of
Economics*, Translated by George Reisman. Edited and
with a foreword by Bettina Bien Greaves (Indianapolis:
Liberty Fund, 2013).
http://oll.libertyfund.org/titles/2427

THE THING ITSELF

◇◇◇◇◇◇◇◇◇◇◇◇◇◇◇

"On 20th anniversary, Dartmouth Review alumni look back,"
The Union Leader (Manchester NH), October 16, 2000.

"Origin of the Expression: 'Blow Smoke Up Your Ass.'"
http://www.todayifoundout.com/index.php/2014/05/ori
gin-expression-blow-smoke-ass/.

O'Rourke, P.J. 1991. *Parliament of Whores*. New York:
Atlantic Publishing.

Plato. "The Republic." In *Great Dialogues of Plato*, translated
by W H. D. Rouse edited by E, H. Warmington and P
G. Rouse. New York: New English Library (Mentor),
1956.

Polybius. *The Histories*. (Internet Archive). Translated by
Hultsch, Friedrich Otto, 1833-1906; Shuckburgh,
Evelyn S. (Evelyn Shirley), 1843-1906
https://archive.org/stream/historiespolybi00hultgoog/his
toriespolybi00hultgoog_djvu.txt

Riker, William H. *Liberalism Against Populism: A
Confrontation Between the Theory of Democracy and
the Theory of Social Choice.* San Francisco, CA: W.H.
Freeman and Company, 1982.

Rose, Derek. 2000. "On 20th anniversary, Dartmouth Review
alumni look back."October 16, P. A9. New Hampshire
(Manchester) *Union Leader*.

Smith, Adam. 1776. *The Wealth of Nations*, Liberty Fund
OLL, http://www.econlib.org/library/classics

Texas State Historical Association, "Handbook of Texas Online," accessed December 16, 2003, http://www.tsha.utexas.edu/handbook/online/articles/view/LL/hcl13.html

U.S. Census Bureau, Census 2000 Redistricting Data (P.L. 94-171) Summary File and 1990 Census. Table 2: Counties Ranked by Population: 2000. Internet Release date: April 2, 2001, accessed December 15, 2003. http://www.census.gov/population/cen2000/phc-t4/tab02.txt

Wald, Matthew, "At Dartmouth, the Right Borrows the Protest Mantle of the Left," *New York Times*, A-14, Feb. 13, 1986.

Weber, Max. (1922) 1968. *Economy and Society*, edited by Guenther Roth and Claus Wittich. Berkeley: University of California Press.

Zakaria, Fareed. 2003. *The Future of Freedom: Illiberal Democracy at Home and Abroad.* New York: W.W. Norton & Company.

THE THING ITSELF

◇◇◇◇◇◇◇◇◇◇◇◇◇◇

◇◇◇◇◇◇◇◇◇◇◇◇◇

PREVIOUS VERSIONS OF PORTIONS OF ESSAYS
(Chronologically)

Munger, Michael. 2004. "Pilgrim's Egress," Parts I, II, and III. *New Sense*. Edited by Madison Kitchens.

Munger, Michael. March, 2005. "The Thing Itself." EconLib, Liberty Fund, Indianapolis, IN http://www.econlib.org/library/Columns/y2005/Munger thing.html

Munger, Michael. January, 2005. "Democracy is a Means, Not an End." EconLib, Liberty Fund, Indianapolis, IN. http://www.econlib.org/library/Columns/y2005/Munger democracy.html

Munger, Michael. November, 2008. "Planning Order, Causing Chaos: Transantiago." Econlib, Liberty Fund, Indianapolis, IN, http://www.econlib.org/library/Columns/y2008/Munger bus.html

Munger, Michael. August, 2014. "How Colleges Fail Liberal Students." *Minding the Campus*. http://www.mindingthecampus.com/2014/08/how-colleges-fail-liberal-students/

Munger, Michael. August, 2014. "Unicorn Governance." *Freeman*. http://fee.org/freeman/detail/unicorn-governance.

THE THING ITSELF

◊◊◊◊◊◊◊◊◊◊◊◊◊◊

Munger, Michael. January, 2015. "Hasta La Victoria
    Siempre." *Freeman.*
        http://fee.org/freeman/detail/hasta-la-victoria-siempre

Michael Munger

◊◊◊◊◊◊◊◊◊◊◊◊◊

Made in the USA
Lexington, KY
20 February 2015